Go Motorhoming
and Campervanning

Go Motorhoming and Campervanning

Special Thanks: We are indebted to the following industry experts who generously gave up their time to proofread this book: Andy Clarke (www.ukmotorhomes.net), Barry Crawshaw, Barry Norris, Dave Hurrell and Gentleman Jack. We are also grateful to Don Madge and the people from companies, organisations, and members of the public that helped us along the way. We are especially thankful to those people that helped to shed light on the numerous moot points discussed in this book.

Editorial Team, Vicarious Books, 62 Tontine Street, Folkestone, Kent, CT20 1JP.
www.VicariousBooks.co.uk
Authors: Chris Doree and Meli George
Contributing writers: Andy and Sue Glasgow
Editors: Chris Doree and Meli George
Editorial assistants: Caroline Stacey and Lauren Smith
Copy editor: Pami Hoggatt
Design and artwork: Chris Gladman Design Tel: 07745 856652

Front cover main image: Thaon Les Vosges, France.

First published in Great Britain by Vicarious Books LLP, 2006. First edition published by Vicarious Books Ltd, 2012. Reprinted with amendments 2013.
© Vicarious Books Ltd 2012.
Copyright © text Vicarious Books Ltd.
Copyright © photographs Vicarious Books Ltd unless otherwise stated.
ISBN: 978-0-9566781-1-9

Readers are strongly advised that all electrical and gas installations and repairs should be carried out or inspected by properly qualified engineers.

CONTENTS

Go Motorhoming and Campervanning

What is a motorhome, a car, a house, an escape? No wonder you've always wanted one. Whether it is the retirement present you have worked so hard for, or a cheap campervan to go on tour, you will love it just the same.

Throughout this book we use the umbrella term 'Motorhome' regardless of vehicle size and origin. Therefore Campervans, Mobile-Homes, Motor Caravans, Recreational Vehicles (RV's), and Camping Cars, are all 'Motorhomes'.

Motorhomes make perfect transport to see the sights or enjoy Mediterranean winters, they can help you find a new life abroad, and they enable thousands of hobbyists to follow their passion.

Go Motorhoming is not a fluffy travelogue but a fact-packed, no-nonsense guide that will turn a novice into a pro. Even the most experienced motorhomer will be inspired to make more of their foreign escapades.

Whatever your calling, your motorhome offers you freedom and spontaneity unrivalled by any other means of travel, always with that reassuring home from home feeling, wherever you find yourself.

Go Motorhoming and Campervanning

La Suze sur Sarthe, France.

Mosel Valley, Germany.

CHAPTER 1 - Understanding Motorhoming

Do people buy motorhomes to go 'motorhoming' or to pursue their interests? Do you know where you want to go, how often and for how long? Why choose a motorhome over a caravan? Perhaps you are reading this book to answer these questions; the good news is that it does and many more. We advise you to read right through to the Summary so that you gain a complete understanding of motorhoming.

Caravans outnumber motorhomes in the UK because most UK campsites are found in rural locations, thus a mode of transport is beneficial and none is more convenient than the car that towed the caravan. Having to decamp your pitch and prepare your motorhome for the road so that you can drive to the local shops or attractions soon becomes a chore. Most British caravan owners restrict their travels to 50 miles from home and few take their caravans abroad but those that do tend to stop on one campsite for the majority of their holiday. Restrictive UK regulations force the majority of campers to stay at official campsites, and this makes a car and caravan more practical than a motorhome. The tables turn as soon as you decide that you mostly want to travel on the continent because many European countries permit the occupants of a motorised vehicle to cook, eat and sleep 'within' the vehicle when parked. DVLA (Driver Vehicle Licensing Agency) registers motorhomes by the old fashioned name, Motor Caravan, which by design is a personal motorised vehicle with self-sufficient accommodation. Caravans are temporary static accommodation with wheels for transportation, and using them is deemed as camping, which may only be done at campsites. Throughout this book we refer to stopping

Caravans outnumber motorhomes in the UK.

There are approximately 10,000 motorhome stopovers across Europe. Sancoins, France.

overnight by the side of the road as Offsite-Parking. Over the decades Offsite-Parking has developed in such a way that officially designated motorhome-parking places, referred to as Motorhome Stopovers in this book, are very common in: France (called Aires), Germany (Stellplätze) and Italy (Sosta). Motorhome Stopovers are mostly located in towns and villages but are also by the coast, alongside rivers and canals, and at ski resorts. The majority of Motorhome Stopovers are simple car parks without a reception or guardian, but most have Service Points where toilet cassettes can be emptied and fresh water drawn. Often both the parking and service is free, with an unwritten rule that motorhomers spend their money locally and stop for no more than two nights. This unencumbered, come and go as you please system is so popular in Europe that motorhomers use Motorhome Stopovers far more than campsites. Chapter 6 fully discusses accommodation options.

Chinese whispers are rife in the motorhoming and caravanning community, so there are plenty of rumours going around and some are so old that they are practically biblical. Over the last 10 years, we have spent more than 1,000 nights parked offsite all over Europe without incident. The biggest concern amongst inexperienced motorhomers is being gassed and broken into at Aires. The College of Anaesthetists has stated in writing that it is not

Motorhome Stopovers often have a drinking water tap and somewhere to empty your toilet.

possible to render someone unconscious in a motorhome: see their statement on page 95. At the time of reprint there was no official record of gas being used during burglary. If you are still unconvinced research the siege of the Russian Dubrovka Theatre on 23 October 2002. Unfortunately, motorhomes, caravans, cars, trucks, and coaches do get broken into at motorway service and rest areas, especially in southern France and Spain. The French word Aire translates to area. Confusingly, both motorway rest

No wonder Motorhome Stopovers are very popular in Europe.

French motorway services are also called Aires. Photo: Maureen Madge.

areas and designated Motorhome Stopovers are commonly referred to and named 'Aires'. Misreporting and misunderstanding of these crimes is common. The fact that the victims were parked at motorway service areas, not official Motorhome Stopovers, has not been clarified. Never park overnight at motorway rest and service areas, even if it has a motorhome Service Point, and be vigilant at all times.

Having decided that you want to tour without constraint, rather than book in and set up on campsites, you can consider yourself a motorhomer. As you travel from place to place, you pick up everything you need to allow you to park for a few days. You then explore the local area on foot, by pushbike or by public transport, so an additional engine-driven mode of transport is unnecessary. If you are adamant that you are only going to stop at campsites then you can consider yourself a camper. The good news is that a car and caravan/tent can be purchased significantly cheaper than a motorhome and are a much more practical option for campsite use. We realise that some people simply do not want to tow, especially a large caravan, or do not have a licence to tow their desired caravan. If you think that a caravan would be more suitable for you, consider attending one of The Caravan Club's towing courses or gain your towing licence.

Maiden Voyage

Travelling by motorhome for the first time can be a daunting experience, but if you are doing so in your own motorhome, you will have already come a long way. Motorhomes are a luxury purchase and only time will tell how frequently you use one, if at all, and whether or not you made a good buying decision. Just about all

A modern VW Camper Van available for hire. www.conceptcamperhire.co.uk

motorhome owners would agree that hiring a motorhome before you buy, especially if you have not owned a touring caravan, is highly recommended. Ensure that you hire a motorhome with a toilet. Before you hire, read the small print and check what costs are incurred for damage. Are there any territorial restrictions, for example GB mainland only? Australian hire companies exclude you from driving down dirt roads unless a 4x4 is hired. The handover may be basic. Ensure you understand how to turn the water and gas on and off, how to fill the water and gas tanks and how to empty the toilet and wastewater. Make up the bed and make sure you know where everything is before you leave the rental company. If something breaks down or gets broken, contact the rental company immediately as they may be able to give advice and suggest where repairs can be made. Always contact the rental company before work is undertaken and keep any receipts. Do make sure you return a clean camper with empty toilet and waste tanks to avoid expensive cleaning charges.

We recommend that you take a trip to France to learn what European motorhoming has to offer. Buy and study the appropriate guidebooks in advance, as these are unlikely to be for sale at the rental office. Stop overnight in campsites of varying standards and at Motorhome Stopovers to get the full experience.

Australian hire companies only allow their 4x4 motorhomes to be driven on dirt roads.

Going bush is quite normal in Australia.

We hired a motorhome in Perth, Australia. After a 20-hour flight and a couple of hours sleep at a cheap hotel, we walked to the hire company adjacent to the airport to collect our motorhome. Having completed the paperwork, we watched an induction DVD and had a very quick handover. From Perth we travelled 1,200km north to Coral Bay in Western Australia. The motorhome gave us freedom to explore anywhere accessible by asphalt road. We purchased a Camps 5 (now Camps 7) book at a camping and outdoor shop and this gave us the locations of serviced parking areas where we could camp out in the bush. This proved to be much cheaper than doing the same trip staying in campsites or hiring a car and stopping at hotels. We saw amazing sunsets and sunrises over the Australian bush and cooked our dinner over open fires.

Hiring a motorhome might seem expensive but will almost certainly save you money in the long run and the experience will probably cause you to choose a completely different motorhome to what you originally thought. Some hire companies offer special purchase deals post hire. A list of hire companies can be found at www.worldofmotorhomes.com/hire-and-rental or check the adverts in motorhome magazines.

An equally viable option to hiring is to buy a budget motorhome that has reached the point where depreciation is entirely down to condition. Therefore, if used sympathetically for a short time there should be little difference between purchase and sale price. This is a great way to find out what you must have but more importantly what you can do without. Buy carefully and you should have no problem reselling. See Chapter 2 for a full explanation. The success of your first trip will depend on your forward planning.

Escorted tours save you the job of planning and provide a reassuring backup. You will meet at a designated place, probably at a port, and then drive your motorhome between pre-planned destinations. You may drive in convoy or self navigate, giving you the freedom to visit places of interest en-route. The tour leaders will be experienced motorhomers as will some of the other people on tour. All will be happy to talk to you and offer help when required. Experienced motorhomers may find that organised tours provide a relaxing holiday or the opportunity to visit places they would not wish to visit alone.

We travelled with GB Privilege on an escorted holiday to the Netherlands to visit Christmas Markets in Valkenburg's caves. Included in the price of the tour were ferry-crossings, maps, campsite fees, entrance to the caves, a bus trip to a neighbouring town market and a communal restaurant meal. We found it stress-free despite staying in a busy campsite in a hectic tourist area. We frequently met people from the tour around the town and markets, which some people found reassuring. The tour comprised first timers and experienced motorhomers, many of whom assisted the first timers in getting everything working and answering their questions. For more information contact GB Privilege www.gbprivilege.com, Tel: 01273 301930.

Adventurous people may find it practical to join escorted tours when undertaking long over-landing trips. Escorted tours provide visa assistance and the necessary support you will need to complete an adventure around the Mediterranean or on the Silk Route to China. Contact Perestroika Tours, a German company that organises various extreme trips annually, visit www.mir-tours.de, Tel: 0049 6746 80280.

Mother Ivey's Bay beach and campsite are busy during the summer holidays.

School's Out For Summer

European holiday hotspots are extremely busy and hot during the summer. Southern Europeans traditionally take the whole of August off work, Scandinavians holiday in July, whilst the French take holidays in both July and August. During this time, campsites by the sea and at any other tourist spot can be full to capacity despite charging peak rates. Conversely, cities can be deserted and the shops shut. Northern Europe is pleasantly warm during August and makes an excellent destination to get away from the madding crowd. Consider visiting northern France, Belgium, The Netherlands, Germany, and northeastern Europe. The Baltic coast offers a completely different beach holiday experience from the Mediterranean. Europeans go back to work in either the last week of August or the first week of September and the campsites take on a ghost town appearance. Most campsites stay open until the end of September and offer cheap rates despite the glorious September sunshine.

The heat during August can be unbearable without, and sometimes even with, air conditioning. Central Europe should be hotter than the UK but the hottest places are southern Spain, Italy, and Greece. Simple heat management techniques can help you enjoy the sunshine without having to

Park in the shade to keep cool during summer.

use air conditioning. Motorhomes are normally white to reflect heat, but strong sunshine causes the internal temperatures to rise quickly and heat both the fabric and contents of the motorhome. Once the sun sets outside temperatures fall, but the motorhome acts as a storage heater so internal temperatures can be uncomfortable at bedtime. Always try to park in the shade and consider where the sun will move. The perfect pitch would have early morning and late afternoon sun, but deep shade during the day. Ideally, your motorhome will be fitted with window blinds, these usually have a silver backing and should be kept shut when parked. Most heat will travel through the windscreen so curtains or blinds on these windows should also be shut, alternatively cover the windscreen with reflective screens. Creating a through draught by opening windows and top vents can be very effective. Remember that all windows and top vents must be closed and the motorhome locked when unattended. Most motorhomes are fitted with three-way absorption fridges and these may struggle to keep contents cool in very hot conditions. See page 63, Chapter 3, for a full explanation. To give your fridge the best chance, always park with the fridge side of the motorhome away from the sun. To escape high summer temperatures, head north and high, ideally to a forested area in the mountains, so that you can keep cool under the trees.

Swimming is a great summer pastime that can provide a much needed cool down. There are excellent swimming facilities at French lakes and many of the municipal campsites are adjacent to swimmable rivers. Norwegian and Swedish fjords often have free recreational areas with facilities such as changing rooms, toilets, barbeque sites, wooden piers, and

Chris cools off in a forest pool.

diving platforms. Even high in the Arctic Circle the water can be warm. Italy is the worst place to go for a beach holiday as most of the beaches are private and only small areas are open to the public, often in the most inconvenient places. In addition to a swimming costume, take water shoes (diving suit material with rubber soles), which are available from virtually every seaside town. Consider taking a waterproof pouch if you have an electronic key fob or don't want keys to suffer water and salt corrosion.

Norway is well worth visiting in June or July as long as you have a healthy budget. Temperatures are similar to the UK with the rain to match, so avoid Scandinavia if forecasters predict a wet summer. If you are lucky and visit during a heat-wave, you will be able to make the most of the Arctic Circle's pristine beaches. Minor motorhome modifications may be necessary, first to protect you from the ever-present mosquitoes, and secondly to ensure internal darkness as 24-hour daylight plays

Norway is a fantastic location even at midnight.
Photo: Andy Glasgow.

havoc with natural sleep patterns. People are often out of bed in the middle of the night so avoid pitching near communal areas, as these can be noisy. The Aurora Borealis, known as the Northern Lights, are not visible in the summer and the Arctic Circle is not suitable for motorhome travel during the winter due to the extreme cold and frozen conditions.

Winter Sun-Seekers

The phrase 'sun-seeker' refers to motorhomers and caravanners who migrate south for the winter. The peak period for winter sun-seeking is January to March but some people start heading south in October. What could be nicer than slowly meandering south in 25°C daytime temperatures, stopping off at deserted beaches whilst the seas are still warm, and witnessing the grape, olive and citrus fruits harvests? Sun-seekers return to northerly countries in the spring, before temperatures become unbearable and the busy tourist season begins. Many winter sun-seekers have proven that Spain can be driven to in a couple of long days. You will need to drive fast and follow the main roads and motorways. We think this is insane. Why exhaust yourself when you can drive the scenic route and start your holiday from Calais?

Chantada wine region in Spain could be visited on your way south.

Camping Bonterra Park, in Spain, is located in the town and near the beach.

Campsites usually cater very well for the long-stay winter visitor, with some sites offering regular events, activities, and transport to the local town or bus/train station. Many campers return year after year, forming strong communities and could be collectively described as a gossip. Campsite location is very important. Ideally there should be good public transport links and the option to walk to a town or vibrant village from the campsite. Advance booking will be necessary at well-located campsites.

Southern Spain is the warmest European location in the depths of winter and the coastal campsites are surprisingly busy. Most days will be warm enough for you to be comfortable wearing shorts. On sunny days, you will be able to sit outside and top up your tan, but it will be cool in the shade and the sea. Expect coastal Spain to be busy. There will be plenty of British company, and there are many places to spend your euros, but be vigilant as handbag snatching and pickpocketing is not uncommon in Spain. Christmas to the end of February is peak season and booking a pitch can be difficult, especially if you have a very large motorhome. There are very few Motorhome Stopovers in southern Spain and the few that exist are in fact basic campsites accommodating only motorhomes. Crowding is not exclusive to Spanish campsites and the Offsite-Parking fraternity complain that it is difficult to find overnight parking. Pre-recession development of the Spanish coast has removed many popular spots and put pressure on the places that remain. Unfortunately, some people abuse

Popular campsites, like Camping la Manga, will be very busy during winter.

the goodwill of locals by staying weeks on end or, worse still, camping rather than parking.

Winter campsites are among the few places at which you might see an American style articulated pickup truck and trailer, known as a fifth wheel, or large American style motorhomes, known as RVs. These large units provide comfortable living space, air conditioning, and large under-floor lockers. If you intend to buy a large fifth wheel or a large motorhome, read Chapter 6 carefully as many campsites cannot accommodate large units. Fifth Wheels are classed as caravans so are not allowed at Motorhome Stopovers.

Consider renting a season pitch if you intend to stay on a campsite longer than a few months. Some campsites offer the option to purchase a pitch on a 99-year lease. Motorhome and caravan clubs organise annual winter rallies to Spain. People find this convenient as their pitches are reserved for them and there are trips and activities organised during their stay. A rally tent provides a meeting place and information point and there is likely to be a book swap box. Contact The Caravan Club, www.caravanclub.co.uk, The Camping and Caravanning Club, www.campingandcaravanningclub.co.uk or The Motor Caravanners Club, www.motorcaravanners.eu, and enquire about their winter rally programmes.

Go Motorhoming and Campervanning

The biggest advantage of heading to Spain, aside from the warmth, is that two other countries, Portugal and Morocco, can easily be visited as part of your winter-sun tour. Portugal is slightly cooler than Spain but has far more charm. The overall situation is similar to Spain and most motorhomes congregate in the Algarve where the warmest campsites are located. Motorhome Stopovers are located inland or on the cooler Atlantic coast. Even though Portugal's coast is much less developed than Spain's, regular Offsite-Parkers have complained that many communal water taps have been turned off and previous parking areas have been blocked off.

Morocco is the warmest and cheapest, easily accessible winter destination off the continent and grows in popularity every year. During the winter, 100 campsites stay open and there are some Offsite-Parking opportunities. Morocco maintains a strong North African identity making it an interesting place to visit. People that have not been to Morocco may feel it is unsafe, but this is unjustified. Crime against tourists is rare because of the harsh penalties. In reality you are far more likely to be a victim of crime in Spain.

Morocco is warmer than Spain during winter. Camping El Barco. Photo: Andy Clarke.

Morocco does offer an off-the-beaten-track destination, but Offsite-Parking is now discouraged. Hundreds of motorhomes once Offsite-Parked unrestricted at Banana Beach. Now guardians take nightly fees and the authorities keep a close eye on things. There is plenty of guarded parking in Morocco, but this is no guarantee that you are allowed to park overnight or that the guardian will guard the vehicle. If you intend to visit Morocco read *Camping Morocco* by Vicarious Books. If you do not want to travel to Morocco independently then GB Privilege can escort you.

Other winter sun destinations include Sicily, Greece, and Turkey. Sicily, and to a lesser degree southern Italy, provide some camping and Offsite-Parking opportunities but the winter temperatures are normally a couple of degrees cooler than southern Spain. A small group of less than 100 motorhomes tour Sicily during the winter. The facilities are very limited and you have to be prepared to be self-sufficient.

Greece is cooler and much quieter than Spain during the winter. You have to take a ferry from Italy to Greece, unless you drive the long way around the Adriatic, but this drive is best saved for the spring. Few motorhomers, and even fewer caravaners, make it to Greece, so do not be surprised if you are on your own most of the time. Offsite-Parking is illegal in Greece and few campsites are open during the winter but they are often inexpensive and quiet.

Standard winter daylight saving does not suit us so we set our clocks forward an hour when we are on the continent and two when in Greece. This helps us to go to bed earlier and naturally wake up earlier therefore we make the most of the limited daylight. There are spinoffs to this time management as you use less battery power when not on hook-up and you get away early so you get to tourist sites or campsites before they get busy.

Turkey is considered a far-flung motorhome destination but is a great place to visit during the winter months. You will experience higher temperatures than in mainland Europe and a different culture. There are campsites open in winter, but, just as in Greece, expect to be on your own most of the time.

The rain will fall in Spain and there is a possibility of snow and frost. After Christmas, most people will consider the sea too cold for swimming. Consider visiting Australia and New Zealand for guaranteed winter sun.

Wave, Wind, And Snow

Motorhomes are popular with sea and mountain sports enthusiasts who chase wind or snow to engage in their sport with optimal conditions. Menageries of motorhomes collect in little groups at secret surf spots all around Europe - testament to the cheap and convenient accommodation these vehicles provide. Heavy equipment could be a problem, so ensure you read Chapter 2 as many motorhomes have sufficient weight capacity for passengers and limited luggage only.

Motorhomes are popular with surfers.

Winter sports enthusiasts should purchase a motorhome designed to cope with very low temperatures. Ski resorts often have high altitude campsites and Motorhome Stopovers so sub-zero temperatures are to be expected. During January and February temperatures will be around -15°C at night, though -21°C is not unusual. Motorhoming in freezing conditions is discussed at length in Chapter 4 starting on page 116.

Camping near the ski slopes at Grimentz. Photo: Andy Glasgow.

Motorhome loaded with leisure equipment.

Hadrians Villa, Tivoli. Photo: Andy Glasgow.

Greek temple, Campana. Photo: Andy Glasgow.

The Grand Tour

There are other ways to tour Europe but none is as convenient, or as effective, as touring by motorhome. You have total independence and the only restrictions will be self-imposed. £1,000 per month is sufficient for two people touring in a motorhome, just £16 per day each! People on tour mostly use Motorhome Stopovers and these are often restricted to 48 hours parking. Not all towns have a Motorhome Stopover; as a result you naturally deviate off the tourist trail.

Following an itinerary helps provide structure to your journey, but often your best memories are not Florence, Rome or Paris but the sleepy town where you drank with the locals. Read a general guide to Europe in advance as this will highlight the best bits and give you an idea of where you want to spend your time. You could easily spend a year discovering France, Germany, or Italy and guidebooks are essential to help you choose where to go and what to see. Several books provide information on the traditional Grand Tour including Kevin McCloud's *Grand Tour of Europe* and Brian Sewell's *Grand Tour*. Literary reads include *Little Dorrit* by Charles Dickens and *A Room With A View* by E M Forster.

Neuschwanstein Castle, Bavaria.

Overlanding

Travelling through most of Europe is not extreme enough to be considered overlanding. European motorhomes are not designed for real overlanding so people convert all-wheel drive vehicles (4x4s) to include living accommodation. Popular overlanding tours include the old trade routes through Asia or Africa.

Expedition Unimog.

Europe is a good place to start your overlanding adventure as you can drive to the Middle East and Asia or head south and across to Africa. This book details everything you need to know about motorhoming in Europe but also read *The Overlanders' Handbook* by Chris Scott. Also visit the following websites: The Silk Route Motorcaravan Network, www.silkroute.org.uk, www.xor.org.uk and www.go-overland.com. Perestroika Tours, a German company, leads various overlanding trips, visit www.mir-tours.de, Tel: 0049 6746 80280.

Morocco could be the start of your overland adventure. Photo: Andy Clarke.

Full-Timing

Full-Timing is the term used to describe people that live solely in their motorhome. Having prepared your motorhome, yourself, and your affairs, you are set free like a fledgling bird. Ask yourself: How are you going to occupy your time when you have no work commitments, family, and social engagements? Where are you going to go? Europe seems very small when you consider that trucks trundle from Calais to the furthest points of Europe within a working week. The perception of Full-Timing is a highly romanticised alternative way of living. The reality is that few people live Full-Time in their motorhomes because alternative lifestyles only suit a minority of people. Motorhomes by design are touring vehicles and medium sized motorhomes are the best compromise between drivability and home comfort when touring. When you live Full-Time in a motorhome, you need space and storage and that means you need something the size of a coach. Unfortunately, Europe is not set up for coach-sized motorhomes and therefore you would have to plan every move. Ask yourself do you want to live in a motorhome or do you want to use a motorhome so that you can see the sights?

> *We gave up our career jobs and set off Full-Time for as long as our budget allowed. In the first 10 months, we clocked up 27,000 miles through 15 countries as we toured to the four compass points of Europe. Long-term touring is demanding both mentally and physically, and we were exhausted after our whistle-stop tour of Europe. We moved much slower for the next two years and changed from a motorhome to a touring caravan, then holiday accommodation. We have learnt that four months is our limit before we need a break from touring.*

Most Full-Timers take extended periods of campsite recuperation, normally through the winter. Some escape their motorhomes and go travelling in other parts of the world or spend some time on organised activities. We recommend that you consider Full-Timing for a year or so, rather than for the rest of your life. If you own property, we urge you to keep somewhere to return to, even if you have to down-size to release capital. Property that is easy to rent is best, as the rent will help fund your trip or pay for repairs and redecoration upon your return.

Isolation can be a problem for all travellers and motorhomers on tour may go for weeks without having a decent conversation. Travelling alone is hard, but even people travelling as a couple suffer isolation; after all, you know

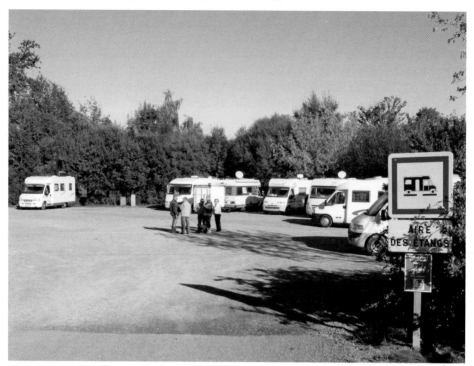

A gossip of motorhomers share information.

everything the other person has done. You will quickly spot sufferers, as they tend to jump out of their motorhome, no matter how bad the weather, eager to speak to anyone with a British number plate. Presumably, this happens to other nationalities because in remote places everyone appears to be the best of friends. Sufferers have to talk at you for around ten minutes with tales of great finds and breakdowns before they are capable of a two-way conversation. To help keep isolation at bay, it is good to socialise and swap information whenever possible, be it with the locals or other campers. Even without foreign language skills, with a little effort you can still have some good times and excellent experiences with the natives or other nationalities. Try to say something in their language even if it is only 'hello' ('hallo' in German). Spontaneous evenings can be great fun and what you learn may set you off in a new direction. All you need is a bottle and some 'bottle' - thankfully one normally brings the other. Non-drinkers will find having a book to swap or any other spurious excuse like "I don't suppose you have a widget like this one" also works well. Most people are happy to chat whether they are touring or static. The very least you should do is let your neighbouring motorhomers know who is in your motorhome as they may act as your security. Sometimes a simple wave from an oncoming British motorhome is exciting. Identifying number plates is hard and it would be much nicer if everybody had a GB sticker on the front, as well as the back of the motorhome. Chances are you will end up bumping into some motorhomers again and again.

Bon Voyage

Whatever type of motorhomer you are, the important thing is to go. There is never a right time, and you never know what will happen in the future. Should you discover that you do not like motorhoming, at least you have tried and if you love it, the quicker you go the better.

Ferries leaving Dover for the Continent.

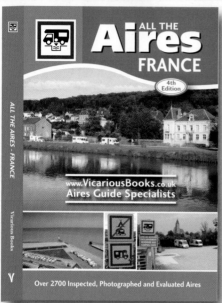

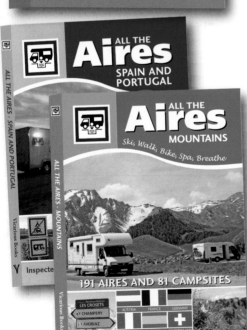

CHAPTER 2 - Your Motorhome

Dr Who's Tardis is the ultimate motorhome, a go-anywhere vehicle with every creature comfort, but is presently unavailable! Earth-based motorhome manufacturers have to work within the constraints of three dimensions but are currently offering over 1,000 new models. When you consider that motorhomes have a 90-year history there is a bewildering selection of makes and models. DVLA register about 9,000 new motorhomes per year in Great Britain. On the 30 September 2012 there were 202,216 taxed motorhomes and 25,127 SORN.

Motorhomes for sale at an outdoor motorhome show.

Getting To Know Motorhome Types

Most motorhomes are built upon or utilise some or all of a light commercial vehicle. Fiat's Ducato has been the dominant base vehicle in recent years, but its siblings Citroën Relay and Peugeot Boxer are also used. All three brands are manufactured in the same SEVEL factory in Italy. Other makes include Mercedes Sprinter, Ford Transit, Iveco Daily, VW Transporter and Renault Master. Fiat and Ford produce special low and wide-track motorhome chassis that offer enhanced ride and handling. Their design means the caravan body floor is closer to the ground. Some motorhomes have an AL-KO galvanised chassis providing similar attributes but also has independent torsion suspension.

Chasis cowl, AL-KO.

Most modern motorhomes have a diesel engine as standard, older, small and American RVs may be petrol driven. Diesel engines offer high torque at low revs so are the most suitable for heavy motorhomes. Diesel is often considerably cheaper than unleaded petrol in Europe so it is worth choosing a diesel engine. Leaded petrol is not widely available on the continent, but the lead substitute added to unleaded fuel is. LPG is available on the continent but not widely in every country. See Chapter 3 for LPG fuel station locations.

Panel Van Conversion, Low Profile Coachbuilt and Traditional Coachbuilt motorhome parked at Kaysersberg.

There are three distinct motorhome types: Van Conversions, Coachbuilt, and A-Class. 'White-Van' Man can deliver anywhere and manoeuvrability is what makes Van Conversions so practical. Coachbuilt motorhomes are the most common conversion and offer the best value for money. A-Class motorhomes are the cream of the crop and can cost as much as a house. Van Conversions are converted panel-vans, sometimes referred to as PVCs. Modern vans have a car-like drive, and despite modest proportions, many

Bailey Approach Coachbuilt with overcab bed.

VW Van Conversion being manufactured at Concept Multi Car Ltd.

Van Conversions are practical for long-term touring. Converters adapt everything from car-derived vans right up to the biggest Mercedes and Iveco high cube monsters. Ignoring length, panel-vans have less internal space than Coachbuilt and A-Class motorhomes for two reasons. Coachbuilt and A-Class motorhomes have upright sidewalls but panel-van sidewalls slope inwards slightly. Coachbuilt and A-Class motorhomes are generally 2.3m (7'7") wide but a panel-van is 2m (6'7") wide or less. Converting a panel-van is awkward because most of the work has to be done within the confines of the van. This is time consuming and therefore increases the conversion cost. Van Conversions have had a revival recently, mainly due to the increased width of modern vans. Two-metre wide vans can have widthways beds long enough, to be comfortable, for people up to 1.83m (6ft) tall. Transverse beds across the back of the van are popular and functional. Often there is a large storage space under the bed or it folds up creating a walkway through the middle. This makes it possible to load bikes or even sheets of plywood for a DIY project. Big, sliding side doors bring the outside in and there is nothing nicer than sitting comfortably inside looking out over a great view.

Left: *This Auto Campers Day Van 3 can be used as a van and a camper. www.auto-campers.co.uk*
Right: *A 1980s Hymer A-Class and a 2008 Pilote A-Class.*

The open sliding door provides a place to sit and enjoy the view. Chris enjoys a view of Western Australia.

Unfortunately, many Van Conversions have a kitchen in the sliding doorway spoiling this fantastic attribute. Opening and closing sliding doors in the dead of the night is noisy no matter how careful you are. Finally, sliding doors let the cold and rain in as soon as you open them. If you feel comfortable with the internal space offered in a Van Conversion, we recommend that you buy one.

Smaller Van Conversions, including the iconic VW camper, are called Campervans and Day-Vans. Campervans are the cool, small, Swiss army camping tool, and just like a Swiss army knife, they have all the gadgets, but they don't really work like the real thing. Some modern campervans have a high top roof but elevating roofs (pop-tops) are more common.

Material sides protect you from wind and rain but offer no physical security. These smaller vehicles are often used as daily transport, but the constrained proportions dictate that facilities have to be small and are often very basic. Showers are rarely installed, so a separate toilet cubicle is unlikely. Refrigeration

Campingplatz Halbinsel Burg, Lake Staffelsee, Bavaria.

will be limited or non-existent. These factors mean that Campervans are rarely self-sufficient and therefore not suitable for Offsite-Parking. Campervans work best for day visits to the beach or a bed for the night when staying out late and they come in to their own on a relaxed campsite where you can spread out your campernalia.

Assorted campernalia and additional sleeping accommodation required by these campervaners in Australia.

Coachbuilt motorhomes best fit the official name Motor Caravan as a caravan body is built upon a light commercial vehicle chassis and the original cab is retained. This is the least expensive way to build a motorhome as much of the conversion is completed before the sidewalls and roof are fitted. Sometimes the caravan body is mounted onto a platform cab rather than a bare chassis. Coachbuilt motorhomes often have a sleeping area over the cab and the roof profile is designed to offer internal space. Some over-cab-bed Coachbuilt motorhomes stand over 3m (10') high so low bridges and tree branches can prove difficult both on the road and in campsites. The law requires that all vehicles 3m or over must display the vehicle height in the cab; you will need to display the height in both feet and metres. Coachbuilt motorhomes are referred to as low profile when the over-cab-bed is removed, thus reducing the overall vehicle height with the benefits of increased fuel economy and a better ride. Low profile motorhomes are the most popular choice with retired French couples.

Coachbuilt and low profile Coachbuilt motorhomes.

A-Class motorhomes look similar to a coach because the donor vehicle cab is not used. The smooth-lined body and purpose-built front end is built upon a bare chassis cowl (engine, electrics, axles, suspension etc, but not the cab). The purpose-built front end has to be designed to be passenger and pedestrian-friendly (complying with European Community directive

Even in a car park we had a grand view from our A-Class Cityvan.

2007/46/EC), an expensive and time-consuming process. To make the most of the extra front-end space the driver and co-pilot seats normally swivel around to become part of the lounge or dining area and a drop-down bed is often found above. Probably the best thing gained is the panoramic view out of the front windows.

Type Approval

Motorhome manufacturers had it quite easy concerning rules and regulations until European Community Whole Vehicle Type Approval (ECWVTA). This has been applicable for cars for many years and affected motorhomes from the 29th April 2009 when it was optional to undergo type approval for new models. From 29th April 2011 any new model launched had to undergo type approval and after 29th April 2012 all new motorhomes must conform to the ECWVTA supporting regulations. Type approval has removed many of the issues discussed below, but it is still a case of caveat emptor, Latin for buyer beware.

Weighty Issues

Prospective purchasers must understand the legal implications when buying a motorhome, especially concerning vehicle weights and driving licence restrictions. To be caught or found to have been driving a vehicle without the correct driving licence or to have overloaded your vehicle and thereby contributed to a fatal accident could well put you in a difficult position. Throughout this book, we stress the importance of not overloading because of the effect this can have upon handling, safety and stopping distances – you have been warned!

When you pack a suitcase for air travel, you know there is a strict luggage allowance and this scenario is no different for motorhome travel. Payload is the term used for the available weight between an unloaded and fully laden vehicle including people and possessions. Chapter 4 explains the amount of payload your motorhome will need for you and your belongings.

Maximum Authorised Mass (MAM) also referred to as: Maximum Vehicle Weight and Gross Vehicle Weight and Revenue Weight on vehicle registration documents. MAM is the legal maximum loaded weight of a vehicle, including all occupants. The MAM should be identified in the vehicle handbook and logbook. The definitive figures are shown on a plate or sticker fitted to the vehicle denoting weight specifications. The plate is

There may be more than one weight plate. Left: AL-KO, Centre: Fiat, Right: Rapido.

normally located in the engine housing and/or the footwells. Often there are two plates, the original from the chassis manufacturer and one from the converter. Converters can have the vehicle weight re-assigned both up and down, but usually only as high as the Maximum Technically Permissible Laden Mass (MTPLM) as specified by the chassis manufacturer, which includes overall weight and axle loadings.

Your driving licence may restrict you to driving vehicles with a MAM of 3,500kg or 7,500kg. For more information see driving licence restrictions on page 34. Motorhomes with a MAM over 3,500kg are often subject to speed restrictions across Europe, see page 214. Some countries charge higher road tolls and others, notably Austria, treat any vehicle over 3,500kg as commercial and expect them to comply with road rules applicable to commercial vehicles. Lowering the MAM of a motorhome to 7,500kg or 3,500kg is possible subject to leaving sufficient payload. The vehicle weight plate will be amended and the DVLA notified.

Motorhomes weighing more than 3,050kg unladen weight are restricted to 60mph instead of 70mph on UK dual carriageways and 50mph instead of 60mph on single-track national speed limit roads.

It would be reasonable to consider that motorhomes built upon a commercial vehicle chassis should have sufficient payload for normal use, enough to prevent illegal overloading. Unfortunately, this is not always the case and it is not as simple as looking at the payload figures printed in glossy brochures, especially on pre type approved motorhomes. Manufacturers' calculations include, or exclude, different items in the unloaded weight that is known as Mass In Running Order (MIRO). MIRO, also known as Kerb Weight, refers to the entire manufactured weight of a vehicle including the equipment required for normal use. At the time of reprint one manufacturer had written that their MIRO calculation accounted for the following; a 75kg (11st 12lb) driver, engine coolants, and 90 per cent of the fuel, gas and water tanks capacity.

Despite the EU calculation of MIRO, most people will 100 per cent fill the motorhome's fuel, fresh water and gas tanks, after all you can't buy a 90 per cent full gas cylinder. For safety reasons, gas cylinders are filled to 80-87 per cent to allow for expansion. Does this mean that gas cylinder weight is calculated at 90 per cent of the 80-87 per cent? We have found examples where only one gas cylinder is included in the calculations but there is capacity for two and aluminium cylinders are quoted instead of steel. Only 75kg is allocated for a driver into the MIRO thus if the driver weighs 100kg, (15st 9lb) the actual payload is reduced by 25kg. Motorhome manufacturers' weight plates may show the pre determined MIRO weight allocated to each model. Thus, any optional extras fitted will increase the MIRO but will not be recorded on the vehicle weight plate, increasingly no MIRO or payload is displayed on the weight plate.

TYP I7870	DETHLEFFS GmbH & Co.KG	
	e1*2001/116*0442*01	
	WDTI7870008386002	
	Blue text not original	Stufe 2
	MAM	5000 KG
08386002	GTW	6000 KG
	1– Front axle	2100 KG
	2– First rear axle	1500 KG
	3–Second rear axle (tag)	1500 KG

Dethleffs three axle motorhome weight sticker.

Before European Community Whole Vehicle Type Approval (ECWVTA), the payloads displayed in different motorhome manufacturers' brochures and on vehicle weight plates were inconsistent. In the previous edition of this book we published four pages of charts that showed data provided by manufacturers in 2005/6 in reference to MIRO and payloads for many motorhomes. Hymer included all 'essential habitation equipment' in their MIRO, allowing for a 75kg driver, 5kg electric cable, 68kg fuel (Ducato), 45kg gas cylinders, and water in tanks at 1kg per litre. In contrast Geist and Mclouis did not include anything, not even fuel. This equates to 293kg difference in the MIRO/payload weights for two similar motorhomes, assuming both have 100L water tanks and the same chassis type.

Shortlist cull

Choosing a motorhome is as easy as one, two, three.

1) Draw up a shortlist.

2) Remove all the motorhomes with less than 500kg payload.

3) Buy one of the remainder.

If your list had no motorhomes with 500kg payload, read Chapter 4 before you buy.

Buyers of pre-ECWVTA motorhomes are advised to ignore any payload figures provided and insist on seeing a weighbridge receipt with the total weight, axle weights and the relevant number plate printed on it. Assuming that no weighbridge receipt was available, we would insist on taking a prospective vehicle to a weighbridge. Stop negotiations if the seller is not willing to weigh the motorhome.

Each axle has a designated maximum weight limit and any vehicle driven on the public highway that is under the MAM but has an overloaded axle is contravening the law. The sum of the axle weights is more than the MAM as this allows for load variation. Axle weights are denoted on the vehicle weight plate and axles are always numbered from front to rear 1, 2, and 3

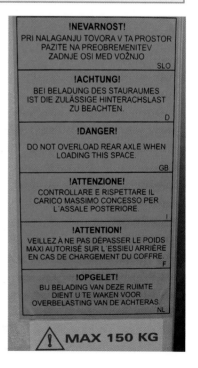

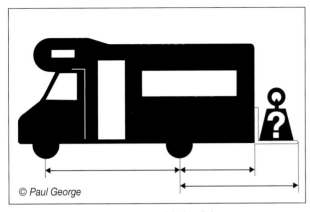

© Paul George

Wheelbase, overhang and user added weight.

when a tag axle is present. Motorhomes are at great risk of exceeding the rear axle loading, especially when built with a rear overhang exceeding 60 per cent. The most likely thing to cause an overloaded rear axle is 200 - 300kg of scooter and rack hanging on the back of a motorhome.

Public weighbridges are common in the UK and Europe. Visit www.chrishodgetrucks.co.uk to find one close to you. Weighing is normally chargeable but the operator may allow you to weigh for free without a printout. First park with all wheels on the weigh plate and record the total weight, then weigh with only the front wheels on the weigh plate to get the front axle weight, repeat for the rear. In a paying situation, weigh the whole vehicle, and one axle, the second axle weight is the remainder of total weight less the weighed axle.

Gross Train Weight (GTW), referred to as Gross Combined Weight in the USA, is a higher figure than the MAM because GTW specifies the maximum combined weight of the vehicle plus a trailer. In theory it is possible to calculate the potential trailer weight by deducting the MIRO from the GTW. Because of the unique modifications made to most motorhomes, converters rarely recommend the maximum trailer weight denoted by the chassis manufacturer. Driving licence restrictions apply.

Being caught driving a motorhome exceeding its MAM, GTW, or axle-loading will, at the very least, result in a verbal warning. Recovery companies clearly state they may not recover vehicles they deem to be overloaded and insurance companies may not payout if they discover the vehicle you were travelling in was contravening the law. It may be possible to raise the payload of a

In the UK, weighbridges are normally manned. In Europe they can be self-service.

motorhome by increasing the MAM. When buying a new motorhome there may be an option to choose a higher MAM, check the technical specification section of sales brochures, but if you do choose to buy a motorhome with a higher MAM expect to wait three months whilst it is built. Increasing the MAM of a used motorhome is more complicated, and may not be possible at all. Often modifications to suspension, brakes, wheels, and tyres are necessary. Contact SvTech for professional advice www.svtech.co.uk, Tel: 01772 621800.

Driving Licence Restrictions

If you passed your driving test in Britain before January 1 1997, unless restrictions apply, your licence will be for category B and C1. This allows you to drive a vehicle with a MAM weight of 7,500kg and a GTW weight up to 8,250kg if towing a trailer. Drivers reaching the age of 70 will lose any entitlement to drive vehicles over 3,500kg, unless a medical is passed and a Medical Examination Report is submitted to the DVLA.

If you passed your test after January 1 1997, you have a category B licence and are entitled to drive a vehicle with a MAM of 3,500kg plus a 750kg trailer. Braked trailers over 750kg may be towed if the combined MAMs of the vehicle and trailer do not exceed 3,500kg but the trailer MAM must be less than the tow vehicle unladen weight. If you wish to drive a vehicle heavier than 3500kg you need to take a C1 driving test. Further information regarding driving licences and online forms are available from www.gov.uk/browse/driving, or pick up a form from the Post Office.

Australians, New Zealanders, Canadians, and Americans can drive a vehicle in Europe with a MAM up to 3,500kg for 12 months from date of entry. It is recommended that you buy an International Drivers Permit before you set off, see page 140.

Pitch fees are sometimes proportionate to size.
Photo: Andy Glasgow.

The 2.1m (6'11") wide Cityvan can feel large in narrow lanes.

Size Matters

The maximum permissible size of a motorhome in the EU is 12m (39'4") long and 2.55m (8'4") wide. A vehicle that has passed an Individual Vehicle Assessment can have a maximum width of 2.6m (8'6"). These measurements exclude awnings, mirrors, ladders, temporary bike racks, handholds, and the like. Most Coachbuilt and A-Class motorhomes measure around 2.3m (7'7") wide. In reality a vehicle 2.3m wide often feels too wide on country lanes and in busy towns. Campsites, road tolls, ferries, insurance, and recovery prices are often fixed up to six metres. A six metre motorhome can comfortably sleep 4-5 people and can be driven almost everywhere.

Bailey Motorhomes are 2.44m (8'0") wide.

Six-metre rule – Six and below the benefits will show, six to seven is close to heaven but seven or more will be a chore.

Some motorhome manufacturers are prone to using the smallest chassis they can get away with. This keeps costs down, but sometimes creates an unnecessarily long rear overhang. Wheelbase is the distance between the centre points of the front and rear wheels. Rear overhang is the distance from the centre point of the rear wheel to the rear of the motorhome. Ideally, the overhang should be less than 55 per cent of the wheelbase to allow for towbars or bike racks, but we once measured a motorhome with a 71 per cent overhang. 60 per cent was the recognised limit and remains a good benchmark but has now been replaced by the following calculation. From a stationary position, when pulling away on a 12.5m-radius circle the rear of the vehicle must not swing out more than 0.8m. Large overhangs are easily scraped on uneven ground, steep ramps and can sag, especially if overloaded. When parked alongside a wall for example do not turn the wheels to full lock then pull off because you will probably tail-swipe the wall, as we once discovered.

Additional Considerations

Should you buy a Left-Hand-Drive or Right-Hand-Drive motorhome? There is no definitive answer, so consider whether you are going to drive mostly in the UK or continental Europe. Visibility is impeded when you are driving the opposite Hand-Drive to the country, particularly at junctions and when overtaking. In addition, the caravan door will open roadside not kerbside. We have owned five Left-Hand-Drive and three Right-Hand-Drive motorhomes. We prefer Left-Hand-Drive motorhomes because most of our travel is continental but have a Right-Hand-Drive car for UK use. Left-Hand-Drive motorhomes generally have lower second-hand value than their Right-Hand-Drive counterparts.

One advantage gained from buying a new motorhome is that it will have a high-rated Euro engine, and therefore accepted into most Low Emission Zone (LEZ) towns. LEZ towns are on the increase across the whole of Europe, so this is

Left or right, which side are you on?

Check your motorhome is winterised before heading to mountain resorts. Photo: Andy Glasgow at Passo d Eira.

something to consider if you intend to drive into large towns and cities. Driving around LEZ towns is generally not a problem as the main routes are not included. If you want to visit a LEZ city, simply stop at an out-of-town site and use public transport to travel in. For more information, see www.lowemissionzones.eu.

Light commercial vehicles latest manufacturing dates. Rollout dates will be earlier. Conversion and first registration could be years later.					
Euro 1	Euro 2	Euro 3	Euro 4	Euro 5	Euro 6
Oct 1994	Jan 1998	Jan 2001	Jan 2006	Sept 2010	Sept 2015
Contact the chassis manufacturer for absolute confirmation. Chassis and engine numbers will be required. Also see http://nl.wikipedia.org/wiki/Light_commercial_vehicle.					

Motorhomes do not have to pass any tests to prove they are suitable for use in cold conditions. The 1998 European standard EN1646 has three grades to define the heating ability of leisure vehicles with accommodation. The standard details how to test a vehicle but there is no obligation to do so. A manufacturer can say the motorhome complies with EN1646 because Grade 1 has no requirement to heat the motorhome or maintain a temperature difference between the inside and outside. Motorhomes do not have to undergo a cold environmental chamber test, but testing is the only way to prove that the stated grade is correct. EN1646 grade 2 and grade 3 tests require the motorhome to be chilled in an environmental chamber so that the fabric of the motorhome and internal space are 0°C and -15°C respectively. The chamber temperatures are maintained at 0°C for grade 2 and -15°C for grade 3 throughout the tests. Using the onboard space heater, the internal temperature must reach 20°C within 45 minutes, and then maintain 20°C or more for two hours. Multiple points are monitored throughout the test. The standard requires that fresh water facilities work, but has no requirement for wastewater.

Grade 2 is good enough for summer use but grade 3 is actually what is required for comfortable habitation. Motorhomes that have passed grade 2 or 3 are not issued with a plate or sticker but may have supporting paperwork. To get definitive answers, contact the manufacturer and request a copy of the test results. The standard does not specify a level of insulation or heater

Is the wastewater tank insulated and will it drain completely.

output. In theory, a motorhome could pass the test with poor insulation if it has a high output heater. Insulation is light but the area covered is large so the weight becomes significant. Walls are a manufacturing compromise area, as they need to be strong, light, thin, and thermally efficient. Thick walls do not guarantee good insulation.

Before heading to the mountains for winter sports, look in your seat lockers or between floor layers to confirm that the water tank is integral. Van Conversions often have under-slung fresh water tanks that are prone to freezing, though some have a layer of insulation. The only way to stop external tanks from freezing is by running a heating element. Double glazed windows in the living area of the motorhome are preferable; check the windows have internal screens or thick curtains to help reduce draughts.

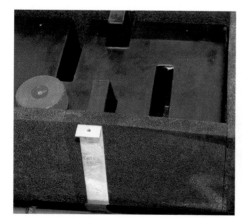

Bailey Approach motorhome insulated water tank.

Bailey Approach motorhome wall insulation.

Don't Buy Inside Out

If men are from Mars and women are from Venus then alienation is possible. When it comes to motorhome buying, gender differences mean that you and your partner could be worlds apart. We have spent many hours at motorhome shows observing and questioning buyers, sellers, and owners. There is no doubt that the majority of motorhomes are purchased by heterosexual couples. We observed that women have a bigger influence in choosing a motorhome. We set about asking sales staff the following question, "Who chooses a motorhome, a man or a woman?" The snap answer was women, but we found that company stakeholders always gave considered responses and tended toward men. Sales staff agreed in general that women choose a motorhome based on the interior space, and that having agreeable furnishings and fabrics are key to a sale. With so many more important elements to consider you must not be a soft touch for the furnishings.

Make up all the beds and check functunality before purchasing.
VW Reimo. www.conceptmulti-car.co.uk

Men tend to look at motorhomes in a different way and are much more interested in functionality, construction, and drivability. We are sure that this is the right way to choose a motorhome and recommend that you agree the size and type of motorhome before you consider the interior. The motorhome should not be bigger than either partner is willing to drive. A bit more workspace here, a slightly bigger bathroom there and a walk-around queen-size bed at the back soon add up.

The Living Accommodation

Compromise is the only word that explains the living situation and, despite countless layouts being designed, there is no easy way to squeeze a kitchen, bathroom, dining room, lounge, and bedrooms into a motorhome. There is no perfect motorhome layout and we have realised that it is best to buy for a specific task and not try to achieve a one motorhome fits all options.

Our Peugeot Boxer Van Conversion was basic but had a 1,000kg payload and a large load space under the rear dinnette. This made it great for taking stock to shows.

We imported this Hymer Camp 55 from Germany when the exchange rate was more favourable.

Over the past 13 years we have owned eight motorhomes and two caravans, each chosen for a task. We bought a 9m American LPG driven RV to go Full-Timing but found it unsuitable for the country lanes we like to drive, so quickly sold it and imported a 6.5m Hymer A-Class. Having returned from our tour of Europe we toured and worked in the UK, so we sold the Hymer and bought a Mazda Bongo day van and caravan. We got fulltime jobs and bought a bigger caravan to live in whilst we were house hunting. We then bought a small Swift Coachbuilt but sold it to fund the launch of Vicarious Books. We imported another Hymer from Germany but this time it was a 1993 Coachbuilt. We used it for Aire inspections but found it too slow. Next, we bought a DIY converted Peugeot Boxer van. We appreciated the extra speed and manoeuvrability but during winter we felt like we were sleeping in a fridge. A PVC that is properly converted will keep you warm and is completely suitable for our needs. In 2008 the Cityvan made by Pilote was the only non PVC motorhome that suited our needs. Over the next four years we clocked up 59,500 miles in the Cityvan and slept in it for more than a years' worth of nights. We never really liked the internal layout and presumably nor did other people as very few were ever sold. In 2012 we replaced the Cityvan with the outgoing Pilote Aventura 600 TGA. The Aventura range replaced the Cityvan and remained the smallest A Class motorhome in production. The Aventura range was widened in 2013 from 2.1m to 2.3m. Presumably Pilote believe that customer's rate internal space more important than drivability.

Our Cityvan was purchased based on its external dimensions and payload.

Some people buy the wrong motorhome, or one that turns out to be too big for them because they think they need to accommodate occasional visiting friends or grandchildren. We suggest that you make guest accommodation a low priority when choosing your layout; after all, you can always put up a tent for them to sleep in.

This section will not tell you the ideal layout – only you can decide that – but it identifies elements that affect your enjoyment of a motorhome. Some designers give more attention to fashion and keeping costs down than functionality but it's the little details make a comfortable and practical motorhome.

Just big enough, is enough.

Bathroom – Some small motorhomes are built without a shower or toilet, which is fine if you always stop at campsites and don't mind trekking to the toilet block. A toilet is essential if you intend to Offsite-Park or use Motorhome Stopovers. However, a large bathroom is an unnecessary luxury as long as you can sit comfortably on the throne and have elbowroom in the shower. According to Dave Hurrell, 75cm is the minimum distance between the sink and anything behind you. People travelling with young children, or less able bodied, may have to make a sacrifice somewhere else to have a large bathroom. Our preference is a wet room designed without a material shower curtain. This design is the most space efficient and is easily kept clean as every surface can simply be wiped down after showering. Prompt wiping down also reduces condensation.

Bedroom/Sleeping – Poor sleep can be a big problem. Roughing it for a week can be fun, but after a month you may not be laughing. The important factors are: access, space, construction, mattress quality, and condensation. Climbing up and down a ladder in the dark is definitely a skill, and clambering over your

Combination fly screen and blackout blind.

partner to get out of bed is less than romantic. A small bed soon becomes cramped after a day or two and, if your feet touch an outside wall, be prepared for cold feet.

The dropdown bed in our A-Class Hymer was a fantastic use of space. It was easier to get into than over-cab beds and could be stowed away fully made up. However,

Check the bed is adequate for your needs and there is sufficient space to add extra bedding.

the dropdown bed in our Cityvan had a serious design faux pas as it has to be extended before use and then covers the hob, so a morning cup of tea cannot be enjoyed in bed. Big rear lounge beds are great, as they can be left made up and the rest of the motorhome functions as normal. Low beds are best in hot conditions. Over-cab beds can be cramped, difficult to get into and very hot, but rising heat is advantageous in winter. We are happy to use an overcab bed, but removed the drop down bed from our Aventura.

Four inches of foam is often not sufficient to make a comfortable mattress. Foam loses its spring with age, but it is inexpensive to replace, especially if the covers are removable. Sprung mattresses are necessary for long-term comfortable sleep, but are rarely standard so invest in having one made. Condensation can occur if there is insufficient ventilation under the mattress/cushions. If a table becomes part of a bed, the laminated surface will cause the cushions to become wet and mildew will attack the cushions if they are not properly aired. Bed slats prevent moisture building up and sprung slats improve comfort. Mattresses and special underlay liners that allow an air gap are available from www.shipshapebedding.co.uk. Seat backs placed directly against cold outside walls also suffer condensation but properly 'winterised' motorhomes will have an air gap.

Check that the windows and vents are screened with both blackout blinds and fly-screens that are mosquito-proof. The best design is a double roller system with the fly screen at the top and the blind at the bottom and the two clip together. The blackout screen needs to be at the bottom so it can be dropped slightly in the morning to let in light but maintain modesty.

Kitchens only need to be just big enough.

Kitchen – Worktops are often cramped and cupboard space limited so ensure there is enough space to prepare a meal, but, as with bathrooms, kitchens need only to be just big enough. Markets and supermarkets are much cheaper and have bigger ranges than campsite shops, so storing food and keeping it cool is a necessity. A fridge and a freezer, no matter how small, are essential, but we find bigger is better. The Thetford domestic-sized, under-worktop fridge-freezer fitted in our Aventura is just the right size and it maintains a very even temperature on all modes, but does use a lot of gas. See page 63 to find out how fridges work. Check that a 230V socket is located so that you can safely boil a kettle. Three gas rings are adequate to cook most meals and a grill is an added bonus. Ovens are not standard in all European motorhomes but are common in British makes and American RVs. Ovens are far from essential, and in every second-hand caravan/motorhome we have bought, they appear to have been unused. Our personal view on ovens is that the loss of storage and additional weight and noise whilst travelling is not worth the occasional roast dinner. There are plenty of worktop electric ovens available and an electric oven is recommended for long-term campsite stays. BBQs and outdoor cookers reduce the need for an oven, but we found that we did not use our gas BBQ when we were Full-Timing, probably because we were constantly on the move and predominantly stopped at Motorhome Stopovers where BBQs are banned.

This Thetford under-worktop fridge is big enough.

Socialising And Lounging – On cold, wet days or mosquito-plagued evenings, you may be lounging or entertaining inside your motorhome for many hours. You will probably want to lounge with your feet up especially when reading or watching TV, so consider where your back and feet will rest. The traditional dinette set-up can prove small and uncomfortable over

Dave Hurrell had a motorhome custom made. A good sofa oposite the Van Conversion sliding door optimises the view.

long periods. L-shaped seating areas (still around a removable table) provide a more comfortable and sociable solution. Seat cushion foam suffers with age. Foam thickness is important but sprung seat cushions prove more comfortable. Dual function design makes sense but is not always utilised. The driver and passenger chairs should swivel to become armchairs, known as captain's chairs, but these are often said to be too high when driving because of the swivel mechanism. The sofa and dining area should become beds without the use of the table, which should be free standing for indoor and outside use. Other design considerations include correct location of TV, lights, and sockets. Both our Swift and Cityvan had only one woefully inadequate and badly located 230V socket.

The socket in our Cityvan was badly located.

This Murvi motorhome has three belted passenger seats.

Belted seats – There are plenty of motorhomes with more berths than belted seats but it is not practical to retrofit seatbelts, so ensure your motorhome has enough belted seats for all your passengers. Because this scenario has not been tested in a court of law, in some circumstances, it is not illegal to carry adult passengers on unbelted rear seats in motorhomes. Realistically it is inadvisable to carry unbelted passengers.

Storage Space – Consider where you are going to store everything. Are there enough lockers and can you access them from both inside and outside? Does the wardrobe have sufficient space? Some motorhomes have garages (large lockers at the rear) designed for bicycles, motorbikes or micro cars. Some are converted to hold pets. Garages are not essential and are easy to overload, but are ideal for

Caravanning inside out?

bike storage as bikes on outside racks get filthy in wet or dusty driving conditions no matter how well covered.

Disabled Motorhomers

Motorhome travel is well suited to people with mobility problems subject to the motorhome being adapted to suit individual requirements. The main advantages are a home-from-home experience with no reliance on third parties if you choose to stop at Motorhome Stopovers. Many campsites have disabled facilities and the most suitable campsite guide we know of is the ACSI DVD. This has a

Dave Hurrell organised his storage to ensure there was space for everything he needed.

searchable database program that you can load onto a laptop. The facilities are explained in detail including: toilets, showers, and access to other onsite amenities. There are 346 UK campsites 'suitable for the disabled' on the DVD and 4,777 across the continent. ACSI inspect all 8,600 sites listed on the DVD every year. You can purchase a copy from Vicarious Books.

Several converters carry out alterations to new and second-hand vehicles. Nirvana Motorhomes has a "try-before-you-buy" scheme for disabled motorhomers and they offer Van Conversions and fully accessible Coachbuilt motorhomes, visit www.simplywav.co.uk, Tel: 0800 3281475. Coachbuilt GB specialise in adapting motorhomes, caravans and holiday homes, visit www.coachbuiltgb.co.uk, Tel: 02476 341196. Motorhomes bought

Wildax can convert PCVs for your needs; including hoists.
www.wildaxmotorhomes.com

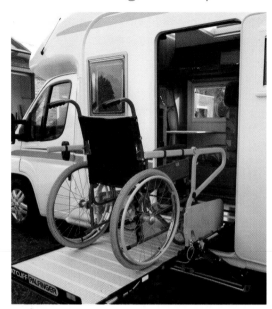

Motorhome adapted and photographed by Coachbuilt-GB.

for use by a disabled person may not be subject to VAT. See VAT Notice 701, http://customs.hmrc.gov.uk, Tel: 0845 010 9000.

MMM magazine includes a mobility supplement every November. Tel: 01778 392496 for a back issue. Also see Queen Elizabeth's foundation, www.qefd.org, Tel: 01372 841100, Forum for Mobility Centres www.mobility-centres.org.uk, Tel: 0800 5593636, and www.wheelgotravelling.info which is a personal site with useful information.

The Price Is Right

Consider both the purchase price and running costs of your motorhome. Factor in insurance, servicing and recovery charges as well as fuel economy. Prices range from £1,000 to over £1,000,000 so it is easy to get carried away, and you will probably find you need to spend more than you originally thought. With some negotiation, £31,000 will buy you a brand new entry-level motorhome. £7,000 will buy a good 20-year-old motorhome. Under £7,000, there are plenty of Van Conversions, VW Campervans and Coachbuilt motorhomes aged 25-30 years.

Motorhomes can cost over £100,000.

Motorhomes have an average life of 25 years and do not depreciate as quickly as cars. Mid-life motorhomes hardly depreciate year to year. In 2003 brand new budget Coachbuilt motorhomes started at £20,000 but they now start £31,000. Second-hand budget 2003 motorhomes are now worth between £12,000 and £20,000.

Motorhomes for sale at The National Motorhome show Peterborough.

Most UK-owned motorhomes are very low mileage. Gentlemans Jack's research for Practical Motorhome found that UK owned Coachbuilt motorhomes average 3,700 miles a year. Europeans tend to clock up high mileage in their motorhomes, mostly because they will happily spend a few hours on the motorways to pop into another county for the weekend. High mileage motorhome can be perfectly serviceable and can be purchased considerably cheaper.

When buying second-hand, age and mileage are no more important than wear and tear. Check the overall condition including the chassis/ underneath, engine, and running gear. Check the seals and trims on the outside for cracks, sun damage, knocks and scrapes. Inside check carpets, cupboards, handles and upholstery. Be aware of any personalisation and

When buying second-hand check for wear and tear.

Personalisation can devalue a motorhome. Painted murals are like motorhome tattoos.

DIY as this often reduces the value. Water ingress is a problem and must be checked for, but can normally be cured. Long-term damp has a distinctive smell, mildew in cupboards is a sign, but an inexpensive damp meter is worth taking along to viewings. Water penetration can cause floors to delaminate; a bouncy feeling is a tell tale sign. Delamination is repairable. Ensure, by testing, that all gas/electricity parts are working. An older motorhome in excellent condition may be preferable to a younger one in poor condition.

Gadgets and gizmos above the basic motorhome specification may not add any value but may be nice to have and may be on your 'must-have' list. Try not to be swayed by extras not on your 'must-have' list and remember they can add considerable weight and, apart from proper alarms, solar panels and awnings, are relatively cheap to add. See 'Preparing Your Motorhome', Chapter 4.

A handful of manufacturers produce the domestic appliances fitted in most European-built caravans and motorhomes, therefore any

Design and function are not necessarily the same thing.

caravan/motorhome retailer should be able to service and supply parts. Parts and repairs on European base vehicles are not a problem. American and Japanese parts can be expensive and difficult to source.

You can look at the MOT history of any vehicle three years old or older at www.MOTinfo.gov.uk, Tel: 0906 1209941, details are provided on the back of MOT certificates. You will need the vehicle registration number and either the document reference number from the V5C registration certificate or the MOT test number from the current MOT certificate. The database goes back to 2005 making it possible to track mileage and see failure and advisory notices. Motorhomes should have annual engine and chassis service, a habitation inspection, and a damp check. Most motorhome owners keep the supporting paperwork, but once a motorhome has changed hands a few times this paper trail frequently goes missing.

Where To Buy

You can do a lot of armchair research on the internet. Visit www.motorhomemarket.co.uk, www.ebay.co.uk, www.gumtree.com, www.autotrader.co.uk or type in 'motorhome classified ads' into your web browser. For European motorhome prices visit www.mobile.de, the German equivalent of Auto Trader, and www.lemondeducampingcar.fr, a French camping car magazine publisher. The 'free ads' papers are a good source of cheaper motorhomes.

Dealers offer choice but may stock motorhomes from only one manufacturer.

Hire fees are often deducted from the motorhome sale cost if purchased after hiring.

Visiting your local motorhome dealers is a good starting point because you will be able to see many different motorhomes, although often only one manufacturer's range. Buying a second-hand motorhome from a dealer affords a greater level of consumer protection than from a private seller. You are likely to pay more from a dealer but you should also get a warranty.

Outdoor motorhome shows attract dealers and manufacturers from all over the country. They will be showing the majority of brands both new and second-hand. There are no second-hand motorhomes at the indoor NEC shows. The September shows may have dealers selling off the current year's stock in preparation for the new models. Shows are held all over the country and are advertised in all the magazines and listed on www.worldofmotorhomes.com. Ticket offers are normally available through the camping/caravan clubs as well as motorhome clubs. If you are going to your first show and it is one of the bigger ones, give yourself two days. On day one look at every type of motorhome from RVs to micro campers, on day two only look at motorhomes that are the size and type that you have decided upon. Dealers should have a wealth of information, so ask plenty of questions, and try to imagine how you will live in the motorhome. Sit in the living space, pretend to cook a meal or have a shower, and make the bed up. Thousands of motorhomes are sold at shows, and no one test-drives them, and if it is second-hand there will be no weighbridge certificate or possibility of taking a prospective motorhome to a weighbridge.

There is no reason why you should not buy a long way from home and you may have to for some European makes and for second-hand motorhomes if you want a specific model. Many dealers have overnight facilities to use whilst motorhomes are in for servicing. If you have niggling problems, these will be more of an issue if your dealer is far away. If you decide to buy new, use the listings in the back of motorhome magazines to get the phone numbers of all the relevant dealers and see what you can negotiate over the phone.

Private sales are often priced much higher than they actually sell for. Response to adverts can be low, so you should be able to negotiate. Comprehensive motorhome warranties are available from the AA, see www.aawarranty.co.uk.

Also read Selling Your Motorhome, on page 61, as it discusses the tricks and essentials for a quick and profitable sale.

Importing From Europe

Importing a motorhome from Europe is relatively easy but the viability fluctuates with the Euro exchange rate. When the rate is favourable considerable money can be saved. Comparatively few European motorhome brands are sold in the UK compared to those that are available from Germany, France and Italy. Germany has the biggest motorhome market, so is the most likely place to import one from. The only problem with buying an unknown brand or model is that it may prove harder to sell back in the UK.

Camper export document, German DVLA equivalent.

Before you import a vehicle from the EU, contact the DVLA to check for any changes to forms or procedures, www.dvla.gov.uk, Tel: 0300 790802. Request either V55/5 for used vehicles or a V55/4 for new. These forms are an 'Application for a first licence for a used/new motor vehicle and declaration for registration'. Also request forms INF106 'Import (Information) Pack' and supporting information. New vehicles can be registered as brand new only if they have reasonable delivery mileage, have not been previously permanently registered, and are a current model or ceased production within the last two years.

Foreign dealers will charge local VAT, Germany applies MWST at 19 per cent. If you are importing a new vehicle, you will also have to pay UK VAT. Once you have the UK VAT receipt you can post it to the dealer for a local VAT refund. Discuss this in advance of purchase.

German dealers will not take personal cheques or bankers drafts, and are not keen on large sums of cash. They prefer you to pay for the vehicle by bank transfer in advance of collection.

Once the imported vehicle is in the UK you have 14 days to register it. A used vehicle, older than three years from first registration in the country of origin, needs to pass an MOT. Some alterations may be required, for example, headlights corrected/changed, fog light on the offside and the speedometer displaying miles per hour graduations that are visible at night.

Left-Hand-Drive vehicles from within the European Community will need a certificate, issued by the Vehicle Certification Agency (VCA), under the Mutual Recognition scheme. This shows that changes have been made to the vehicle, making it suitable for use on British roads. Motorhomes manufactured prior to 28 April 2012 are exempt from VCA procedure. So motorhomes that do not require an MOT may be required to be taken to your local DVLA office for inspection.

Motorhomes that have ECWVTA will have a certificate of conformity and a copy will be needed. Motorhomes without ECWVTA are exempt from SVA tests. Your local DVLA office may request an inspection of the vehicle.

The following information needs to be sent or taken to your local DVLA office:
• V55/5 or V55/4.
• The MOT certificate, if the vehicle is more than three years old.
• The original copy of UK vehicle insurance certificate.
• A utility or bank statement.
• Personal identification: passport or driving licence.
• The export papers including the equivalents of the UK V5C Registration Certificate, that shows the date of first registration.

Vehicles over six months old which have travelled more than 6,000km (3,750 miles) will not be subject to VAT and will be self declared on form VAT 414. New vehicles are subject to VAT and must be declared on form VAT 415. Vehicles imported from outside the EU need form C&E 386; these are required by HM Revenue and Customs for a vehicle of any age, personally imported, to assess any VAT due.

• All imported vehicles need to be stored off the public highway until registration is completed.
• UK residents are not allowed to use non-UK registered vehicles on UK roads.
• Fully comprehensive insurance is not available during the importation of vehicles across mainland Europe. Some companies offer insurance against the chassis number once it reaches the UK. Currently the only satisfactory solution is to have the vehicle delivered.
• If this all sounds like too much effort or risk Bundesvan will assist you through the whole process, see www.bundesvan.co.uk or call Nick on 01803 606335. The key advantages offered are no insurance risk on the drive back to the UK, no foreign money transfer, no double VAT on new vehicles.

German temporary exportation number plates.

John Kelly's self-build. SBMCC member.

Build It Yourself

Self-building a motorhome can save you money and you can create a bespoke vehicle for your desires or needs. The first time you use it will give you a real sense of achievement. The reality is that building a motorhome will be difficult and extremely time consuming and should only be taken on by people with a history of completing projects.

Three months is the minimum build time. £5,000 will fund a budget conversion. Purchasing an accident-damaged caravan is a good way to aquire many of the parts that you will need.

Most people convert a panel van as this is the simplest option. To re-register the vehicle as a Motor Caravan with the DVLA it must pass a 'reasonableness test' to prove that it is a 'motor caravan' which is classed as "a special purpose M category vehicle constructed to include living accommodation which contains at least the following equipment: seats and table, sleeping accommodation which may be converted from the seats, cooking facilities, and storage facilities. This equipment shall be rigidly fixed to the living compartment; however, the table may be designed to be easily removable."

Self-build kits can reduce workload, leaving you to do the bits you are interested in. Alternatively, commission a company to build your motorhome. Ensure you specify in writing what you require in as much detail as possible. Specify exact products to be used and detail the finishes that you would like. This is the only way to prevent a difficult situation if the finished motorhome does not live up to your expectations. Keep in mind that self-build motorhomes will not achieve the same resale price as a recognised brand.

John Kelly, member of the Self Build Motor Caravanners Club, www.sbmcc.co.uk, detailed his motorhome self-build costs.

8 year old, high mileage, extra long wheelbase Iveco Daily 35 s11	£,2600	12v cable (new)	£32
		Replacement cab roof lining (new)	£72
Crash damaged, 4 year old Avondale Osprey caravan	£2,000	Fresh water tank (new)	£40
		Grey waste tank (used)	£20
Collecting caravan	£70	Bicycle rack (salvaged used)	£0
Timber and ply (new)	£360	Bicycle rack repair and fittings	£37
Replacement driver and passenger seats (used)	£42	Water inlet and pipe (new)	£22
		Mains hook up inlet (new)	£14
Passenger seat swivel base (used)	£25	Sealants and glues (new)	£67
Seat adapter plates (new)	£20	Screws and fixings (new)	£64
Sink and drainer (new)	£100	TV/DVD (new)	£110
Leisure battery (new)	£65	TV aerial (new)	£60
Truma 'warm air' heater (used)	£150	Aerial mounting pole (new)	£13
Shower tray (new)	£25	Awning light (new)	£25
Shower and W/C wall cladding panels (new)	£110	Spare wheel cover (new)	£18
		Van graphics	£50
Shower curtain (new)	£8	Carbon monoxide alarm (new)	£28
Shower mat	£10	Smoke alarm (new)	£6
Mini Heki rooflights (new)	£160	Fire blanket (new)	£15
3 LED ceiling lights (new)	£40	Fire extinguisher	£12
Small fluorescent strip light (new)	£15	cupboard & under seat storage bins	£32
Rockwool wall insulation	£20	Angle iron for water tank brackets	£18
Carpet for wall and ceiling covering (new)	£80	12v light switches	£18
		Cab floor carpet	£20
Floor insulation boards (new)	£18	Pressure activated water pump	£68
Floor vinyl (new)	£40	Inverter	£38
Fiamma awning fixing kit	£48	Step edging plate	£14
Fiamma wind out awning (used)	£180	Table leg and table mounting bar	£20
Damaged caravan awning (to make 'safari' room)	£50	2 x 10 litre drinking water containers	£16
		Silver screens	£60
Kitchen worktop (new)	£35	**Conversion cost**	**£7,385**
Replacement toilet cassette (new)	£60	Overhaul van brakes	£250
Gas fittings (new)	£20	Sales of surplus caravan parts, windows and heater	-£150
Cooker repair	£25		

Anyone considering building their own motorhome should read *Build Your Own Motorhome* by John Wickersham, available from www.Vicarious-Shop.com and visit the Self Build Motor Caravanners Club website. Other useful websites include: www.rainbowconversions.co.uk, www.deepredmotorhome.com, www.charlesandson.co.uk, and www.magnummotorhomes.co.uk.

The Buyers Checklist

Few sellers will give you an in-depth description about their motorhome unless you ask the right questions. You can save yourself wasted journeys by asking the following questions, preferably over the phone. The first question is a good warm up before the interrogation begins.

- Please describe the layout of the motorhome starting from the cab. Are the cab seats captain's chairs and do they swivel? Is there a separate bathroom with toilet and shower? Where are the beds and what size are they? Is the floor carpeted and is it removable?

The payload of the 3,500kg Roller Team Box is 510kg, with the rear garage limited to 400kg.

- What is the overall size of the motorhome?
- How long have you owned it and why are you selling?
- How often and where did you use the motorhome? How many miles has it done, how many have you done in it, and how many in the last year?
- Is it diesel or petrol? What capacity is the engine, is it powerful enough uphill and on the motorway? How many miles to the gallon? Does it use any oil?
- Is there any damage to the vehicle, has it been accident repaired? Is there sun damage?
- What repairs have been done? Has it had a new exhaust? How old are the tyres?
- What is the MAM and payload? Does the MIRO weight include full fuel tank, driver, full water tank, and full gas cylinders? If the seller is unsure or blasé then the likelihood is they may have been using it overloaded.
- What service history does it have? Does it have its original documents (manuals)? When did it have its last MOT, engine chassis and habitation service and by whom?
- So that you can look at the MOT history ask for the vehicle registration number and either the document reference number from V5C registration certificate or the MOT test number from the current MOT certificate.
- Is anything not working properly or broken?
- Is there, or has there ever been, any damp?

- What is the interior condition like? Where are the marks, scuffs, or wear? How worn are the cushion covers? Is the foam starting to show signs of age? How clean/worn are the carpets?
- Has it had any DIY alterations or paint jobs?
- What kind of heating system does it have?
- What hot water system is there? Does it run on gas, electricity, or both?
- How large is the water tank? Where is it located and is any filter system fitted?
- How does the toilet system work and how much capacity do the toilet and wastewater tanks have?
- Is the fridge compressor or 3-way? Does it have a freezer compartment?
- Are there blinds and fly-screens on the windows and top vents?
- Is there enough storage space? Are there any externally accessible lockers?
- What capacity is the leisure battery in amp hours? How old and how easy is it to access? Are there any 12v sockets? Does the motorhome have electric hook-up? Is the cable included? Where are the internal plug sockets located and how many are there?
- What security features does it have, i.e. locks and alarms?
- What add-ons or extras come with it?
- How many and what size gas cylinders does it take? Are the gas cylinders included?
- Can you arrange for us to take the motorhome to a weighbridge during our test drive?
- What warranty is included and what are the conditions, i.e. return to base or Europe-wide?
- How did you come to the advertised price and have you since reduced it? Only ask this question toward the end as it may affect the way a seller answers further questions.

Left: Check the bed construction and storage space.
Right: Check the ground clearance. Steps and pipes can catch on uneven ground.

We have found that a private seller, who answers these questions confidently and willingly, is selling a genuine motorhome in the condition described. The main problem will be convincing them that they should sell you the motorhome at the price you think its worth. When the alleged owner answers questions poorly, is evasive or repeatedly says, "it's a good runner - a really nice camper" then the chances are you will see a different motorhome to the one you had in mind. Expect to be on the phone for at least 20 minutes and, unless you are completely sure, don't bother driving a long distance to see a private sale motorhome. Equally, don't fall in love with it before you've seen it. One final point, people prefer you to be honest, so whether on the phone or at a viewing, if it is not right for you stop there and tell them so and why. A departing, "I will think about it" when you have no intention of buying it is very frustrating for the seller.

Seriously consider having any prospective motorhome professionally inspected. Motoring recovery organisations and several national companies will carry out base vehicle visual inspections but will not be able to comment on the 'caravan' elements. The best option, if possible, would be to take it to a motorhome service centre.

Motorhomes for sale at The National Motorhome Show, Peterborough.

2001 Nissan 2.2 diesel 5speed manual, midi size coachbuilt, new Nu Venture body in build now, toilet compartments with cassette toilet
£18,500

Selling Your Motorhome

The starting point of any second-hand sale is working out how much the motorhome is worth. Depreciation is inevitable, but how much depends on age and condition. Do not overprice your motorhome, as it will probably waste both time and money. Private sale motorhomes, no matter what value, sell for £2,000-£3,000 less than comparable motorhomes advertised on dealer forecourts. The Warners' magazines – MMM, Which Motorhome and Caravan and Motorhome Mart – run the same classified adverts. These are also displayed online at www.outandaboutlive.co.uk. According to Carly from Warners, most motorhomes are sold within three months, but each time the advert is renewed the sale price is reduced by £1,000. Motorhomes priced on the cheap side of realistic sell very quickly, often from the website before the magazines are printed. Motorhome dealers will often negotiate a price over the phone, but they will err on the side of caution. Local dealers will probably want to see your motorhome either at their premises or yours. This gives them the opportunity to assess a fair price but also to charm you. Once you have a trade price you can compare it with private and dealer adverts for similar motorhomes. Remember the dealers mark up between £1,000 and 50 per cent. MMM publishes a six-part second-hand price guide, but this only shows dealer forecourt prices of available models. Part-exchanging is unlikely to be the most economical, but offers a simple solution. Additional equipment does not necessarily add value but may make your motorhome more sellable. Remember that any DIY, repairs or personalised interior/exterior design will probably lower the value if it does not appear to be a professional job.

Clean the motorhome thoroughly inside and out (dealers do) and remove anything that is not included in the sale. Provide as much information about the vehicle as possible, and have it MOT tested. If you are selling from your drive, make the area presentable and park so the vehicle can be inspected on all sides. Finally, don't warm up the engine before a viewing, as buyers will be suspicious about its starting ability. Batteries are affordable, so replace if necessary.

Clean your motorhome roof before you sell it.

Most prospective buyers have an idea of what they want, but may not know much about your specific model. Use the Buyers' Checklist on page 58 and try to answer the questions whether they are asked or not. It is worth asking them over the phone what models they like, and how they intend to use the motorhome. We always follow this process because it is not worth wasting everybody's time viewing an unsuitable motorhome. Where should you advertise? We have had good responses from the free classifieds websites, so try these first. We have had some success from

Auto Trader. When selling the endless sales calls from people wanting to send free information or having buyers looking for a "Winnebago campervan" are frustrating. Don't be discouraged by callers who arrange to view only to cancel on the day. Remember you also had no idea what you wanted at some stage.

Meaningful test drives are essential.

Test drives are essential but it is unlikely that a prospective buyer has sufficient insurance cover, if they say they have ask for proof. If you, as a seller, have fully comprehensive 'any driver' insurance, check the small print for age or penalty restrictions. Personally, if a buyer with relevant insurance really wants to drive we would take them to a deserted car park. Even from the passenger's seat it is possible to assess the vehicle condition, and the way it has been driven. Look for clutch travel and whether the driver uses the pedal as a footrest. Listen and watch for smooth gear changes, including reverse. Take the vehicle on a dual carriageway, up a steep hill, and on twisty roads, all of these will give an overall impression of running condition. In addition, reverse up a steep hill to ensure there is no clutch judder. Take the opportunity to visit a weighbridge and find out exactly what payload is available. Finally, people do steal vehicles whilst on test drives or viewings, so stay with them at all times when they have access to the keys.

Further Information

Auto Trader has detailed information with tips for buyers and sellers at the start of its magazines and online at www.autotrader.co.uk. This information details everything from how to write your advert to what questions to ask and security checking the vehicle for damage, theft, or outstanding finance.

CHAPTER 3 – Life Support: An Idiot's Guide

Motorhomes have everything required for a day or more away from civilisation, and the more you know about how things work the better your trips will be. This chapter could be considered an induction for motorhome occupants, and is written in the KISS style, Keep It Simple Stupid. Some subjects are so important that they are explained in depth so that you can make the most of your motorhome. To bring things into perspective real life examples have been provided. Onboard utilities include electricity, gas, and water, and these can last up to seven days with frugal use.

Switched On

Although water is fundamental to life, water will not flow from motorhome taps unless there is a source of electricity. Most motorhomes have three interlinked electrical systems controlled by a panel, located in the living area. The base vehicle has a 12V engine starter battery that powers all the driving related electrical items. The habitation area has its own wiring system and 12V battery known as a leisure battery. This is essential to prevent the engine battery becoming flat. The habitation area also has a 230V mains circuit that is usable when a mains supply is available.

To understand how the three electrical systems are interlinked we will look at how a 3-way absorption refrigerator operates. Domestic fridges and freezers use a compressor to propel the refrigerant liquid around the metal tubes; you have probably heard the motor running. Few motorhomes are fitted with compressor fridges because of the noise, but also they can consume a considerable amount of 12V electricity.

This Truma control provides simple, accurate 12V and water levels. In addition, there are gas and electric heater controls.

Go Motorhoming and Campervanning

A 3-way absorption fridge requires a heat source to drive the cooling process. Heat causes the refrigerant to expand and the pressure pushes the refrigerant around the system, this is known as a heat pump. Three energy sources provide the heat, either a 12V or 230V electrical element or by burning gas. Old motorhomes may have fridges than can run on gas without any electrical supply, but typically there will be a control panel managing the fridge and this will draw power from the leisure battery.

When the vehicle engine is running, a 12V heating element provides the heat source for the fridge. This element requires a lot of power, so can only be used when the alternator, (a small generator driven by the engine) is running. The alternator normally charges the engine battery, but has spare capacity. A fridge-control relay (an automatic switch) prevents power being drawn by the fridge from the leisure or engine battery when the engine is not running. A second relay allows the leisure battery to charge when the engine is running. Both batteries charge up to 14V, but the leisure battery may take several hours to fully charge. The fridge has a second heating element powered by 230V electricity and this heats up when you hook-up to the mains. A battery charger also operates when hooked-up, and this charges the leisure, and sometimes engine, battery.

Compressor fridges are suited to expedition vehicles which are driven all day. Sometimes these fridges are fitted in Van Conversions. Compressor fridges should out-perform standard 3-way absorption fridges in hot climates, though ours have worked fine on gas in temperatures up to 37°C. If your fridge does not perform well in hot climates, and you have confirmed that it is correctly installed, a low consumption 12V computer fan can be used to increase airflow through the top vent. Compressor fridges operate solely on 12/24V and this is fine if the leisure battery is receiving a charge because the motorhome is hooked-up to the mains, or the engine is running. When an under the worktop size compressor fridge is running, but no alternative power supply is available, it will flatten an 110Ah leisure battery within one and a half days. Additional leisure batteries can be installed but bear in mind they weigh between 25 - 30kg each.

Banner leisure battery.

Most onboard facilities require 12V to operate, including the water pump, lights, and the heating system. Available power is determined by the capacity of the batteries, their condition and charge state.

Motorhomes normally have lead-acid batteries (wet batteries) for both engine starting and leisure use. Assuming there is no problem ventilating the flammable gasses produced when charging wet batteries there is no point buying expensive gel batteries. Gel batteries do not produce gas and are spill proof so are perfect for boats. Absorbed Glass Mat (AGM) batteries are built for extreme use applications such as powering forklifts and golf-carts.

Starter battery construction enables high energy, rapid discharge, and quick recharge. Repeated slow or over discharge is likely to degrade the thin lead plates. Leisure batteries have thicker lead plates and extra reinforcement to enable frequent deep discharge without damage. When you buy a leisure battery make sure it is labelled in accordance with directive EN50342. See the photos for correctly labelled leisure batteries.

Leisure battery capacity is rated in ampere-hours (Ah). This would suggest that a 100Ah battery should be capable of delivering one amp for 100 hours. Batteries give up more power when discharged slowly and less when rapidly discharged, this is known as Peukert's law. Correctly labelled batteries display the 20-hour nominal capacity. The capacity is determined by three controlled discharge tests at three different amp loadings. The battery voltage is monitored and the test stops when the voltage drops to 10.5V.

This Banner leisure battery displays three amp hour ratings.

This Varta leisure battery displays two amp hour ratings.

Go Motorhoming and Campervanning

You can only know what size leisure battery you need by calculating the number of Ah you think you will use between charges. To do this, work out the amperage of all the items you will use (or would like to use) and for how long. Amps can be calculated by dividing power (watts) by voltage, for example, a 1,000W / 230V fan heater runs at 4.35A, 1,000W / 230V = 4.35A. If the fan heater could run on 12V it would use 83.33A per hour! - clearly a problem if only one 75Ah battery is available. Furthermore the higher the load, the less Ah are available as can be seen by the three figures quoted on the battery label. You can find an online calculator at www.bannerbatterien.com. In reality, most motorhomes are fitted with one 75-110Ah leisure battery, so if you divide the figure you had previously calculated by 10 that'll be the size of battery you will be able to have. A second battery can be run in parallel, but must be properly installed, fused, secured, and vented. The basic rules are that the batteries need to be the same age, type and capacity. They are connected together positive-to-positive, negative-to-negative. This type of connection makes the two batteries behave as one, but the charger will stop once one of the batteries is fully charged. Therefore, it is no good connecting a 75Ah to a 100Ah battery because the 100Ah battery will never fully charge. When two equal capacity batteries are run in parallel both should reach full charge unless one develops a fault reducing its capacity.

According to manufacturers, the optimum operating temperature for a battery is around 27°C (80°F). Available battery power reduces approximately one per cent per 1°C fall in temperature. Therefore, at freezing point a battery's capacity reduces by approximately 27 per cent.

Our recommendation is that standard 110Ah lead acid leisure batteries are suitable for most motorhome and caravan users. They are far cheaper than AGM or gel alternatives and, as long as they are looked after, will perform well for several years. Keep lead acid batteries topped up with demineralised water and charge occasionally during layup periods as a battery can lose up to 1 per cent charge per day even without taking into account drain from clocks or

Two 100Ah leisure batteries connected in parallel.

alarms. People who will always hook-up to the mains, or will only stop a night or two, need only buy a 75Ah capacity leisure battery.

Lead acid batteries do not store electricity but create electricity by transfer of ions across the electrolyte between the lead plates. This process is reversed during charging. To keep a lead acid battery in top condition it is necessary to apply 14.4V or more during charging. Charging at 14.4V or slightly more has a rejuvenating effect, but as a by-product hydrogen gas and oxygen is produced, which is vented outside for safety. To replace the lost hydrogen and oxygen demineralised water (H_2O) should be periodically added to the battery cells.

Mains-powered battery chargers are normally specific to battery type because most gel batteries must not be charged over 14.4V to prevent gassing. Battery chargers can have sophisticated charging regimes and the better the charger the better the charge. In reality, new motorhomes are likely to have adequate chargers fitted. A cheap starter battery charger is unlikely to perform as desired when used to charge a leisure battery. The charge rate in amps should be 10 to a maximum of 20 per cent of the batteries Ah capacity, i.e. 7.5A for a 75Ah battery and 10A for a 100Ah battery.

Battery to battery chargers are sophisticated intermediaries that work when the engine is running. Initially, they boost the normal 14V produced by the alternator so that the leisure battery can not only be fully charged but also charge in a shorter time. Several lower voltage charging regimes are applied during the process to achieve full charge. This type of charger would be a valuable asset to people that rarely use mains hook-up and stop for long periods with short driving time between stops. For further information visit Conrad Anderson's website www.conrad-anderson.co.uk, Tel: 0800 2790085 and Roadpro's website www.roadpro.co.uk, Tel: 01327 312233.

Inverters convert 12V DC battery power into 230V AC mains equivalent voltage. Inverters are

Inverter powering netbook.

most efficient at maximum capacity and efficiency drops quickly as the load reduces, so do not buy one with more capacity than you need. We recommend you write a list of the items that you wish to power and speak to a specialist before choosing appliances or an inverter. Many motorhomers use inverters to run their satellite systems or laptops, but there are many 12V appliances available ranging from kettles and hairdryers, to televisions and microwave ovens, so consider these before opting for an inverter. Using appliances with a higher capacity than the 12v DC system can cope with, may result in a blown fuse or cables and sockets overheating, this in turn could damage the appliance or start a fire. We recommend a short dedicated connection between the leisure battery and inverter. Sterling Power Products Ltd specialises in inverters, visit www.sterling-power.com, Tel: 01905 771771.

12 Volt Electricity Consumption – The Reality

One 75Ah battery powering only the water pump and lights when necessary, will have sufficient power for a pitched week during the summer. The longest we have solely relied on one 110Ah battery between charges is two summer weeks, without TV. People touring that drive every few days should find they charge their motorhome batteries sufficiently without the need of electric hook-up. We monitored 298 continuous days away, during which we hooked-up for 86 nights. We would have hooked-up for only 11 nights had electricity not been included in campsite fees. We are not alone in this usage as most people we have met that are touring followed the same practices.

Electric Hook-Up

Most UK campsites provide 16A electric hook-up, whereas hook-up at campsites in mainland Europe can be as low as 3A. Some campsites offer a choice of hook-up, rated at 6A, 10A, or higher, and you are charged accordingly. When paying for mains electricity, it is worth getting value for money, but there is no point carrying high power appliances that could trip the supply. Items that are worth their weight are: a low watt kettle, a cooking ring, and a dual function fan heater/cooling fan, everything else is a luxury you could take if you have weight and space available.

Any electrical appliance that has a heating element is likely to be rated at 1,000W or more and, as previously discussed, a 1,000W device runs at 4.35A (1,000W/230V=4.35A), thus cannot be used when hooked-up to a 3A

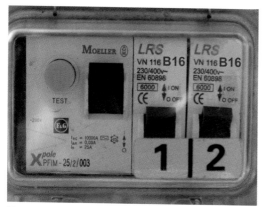

Two 16A circuit breakers, one RCD.

current. You should be able to run the motorhome fridge from a 3A supply and be able to plug in low watt devices such as a laptop computer. Charged leisure batteries are maintained using a low current charge, but the battery charger may trip the electrical supply if the batteries are flat and require a high input charge. Onboard water heaters that have a mains element draw about 2.75A.

Thermostatic portable heaters often have step heat/power levels. The picture of the heater control knob with the three power consumption settings shows the Glasgows' foolproof way of preventing circuit breakers from tripping. You can easily see what capacity supply is available by looking at the circuit breakers. Look at the picture above, this shows a small distribution board with trip switches that are typically found on campsite bollards. In this instance two 16A supplies (hook-ups) are available and are numbered 1 and 2 for identification should one trip. The sockets were also numbered 1 and 2. Circuit breakers are designed to trip if the draw of amps exceeds the breaker rating. Look again at the picture. You can see B16 printed on the two circuit breakers, the B may be a C, but the important point is that the 16 represents 16A. This may be a 3, or a 6 with the amps respectively. The switch to the left of the circuit breakers is a residual current device (RCD). The RCD would trip if someone received an electric shock or a faulty device was used, often a kettle or a heater.

Most of Europe distributes electricity at a nominal 230V. Appliances usually display a label denoting electrical specifications. Most labels show the watt value so it is worth remembering that a 16A supply provides 3680W, whereas a 3A supply provides 690W. The calculation is volts multiplied by amps equals watts, (230V x 16A = 3,680W). A typical domestic kettle draws approximately 2,785W.

Three power settings on the Glasgows' heater.

Expect and be willing to share free electricity at Aires.

at 230V, a low consumption kettle can consume as little as 120W. Therefore you would need over 10A supply to use a domestic kettle, but less than 3A for the low watt equivalent. Microwave ovens consume up to two times the watts at start-up, for example, a 700W microwave requires 1,400W when it starts up.

Amps	Watts	Amps	Watts
3A	690W	10A	2,300W
5A	1,150W	13A	2,990W
6A	1,380W	16A	3,680W

Motorhome Stopovers that offer electricity often have insufficient sockets for demand and when electricity is free it is uncommon for there to be more than one socket. Normally people share the supply but the way this is done is potentially unsafe. Often in these situations, the circuit breakers are unavailable to the users and the supply cannot be reinstated if a circuit breaker or RCD is tripped. If you look closely at the photo above you can see one socket is shared by three motorhomes, although this situation is less than ideal it is fair. The photo was taken at a free French Aire and we were disappointed to see that the other end of the hook-up cable that is secured in place by silver duct tape was plugged into a UK registered RV, not only that, but it was parked in an area that clearly excluded motorhomes.

Multiple motorhomes sharing one plug socket.

Continental Europeans commonly use long domestic extension cables to plug into the mains. In the UK, most people use a 25m leisure cable but 25m may not be long enough on some European campsites. Leisure cables are not designed to be driven over, but are fitted with blue industrial plugs designed to be used outside. The blue socket identifies the source to be 230V. European campsites and Motorhome Stopovers may not have blue sockets, often providing the domestic socket of the country. A mini extension, with a leisure socket one end and a continental two-pin plug the other, is a necessity. By attaching a domestic plug it is no longer rain proof and people often attempt to make the connection watertight by encapsulating it with a plastic bag taped with duct tape.

Reversed polarity is the term used when the live and neutral wires are connected to the wrong terminal, i.e. live to neutral, neutral to live. This is rare in the UK, but dangerous if you tamper with any socket, switch, light fitting, or any wiring. Reverse polarity is common in France, but is often disregarded by foreign motorhomers because their electrical wiring, sockets, switches, and appliances are designed to be used with reverse polarity. Some motorhome control panels correct polarity and others have a light that identifies reversed polarity. Best practice is to test the socket before you hook-up and you can easily test polarity with a plug-in detector. These detectors also identify if an earth is present. For safety reasons do

Camping la Manga all correct LHS.   *Camping la Manga reverse polarity RHS.*

not plug-in if no earth is present. Polarity can be altered in two ways when using French or blue plugs. If you are competent, you can re-wire the plug's live and neutral on-site or carry a second short extension with live and neutral wires already reversed. Reverse polarity will not damage your motorhome electrical systems, appliances, computer, or TV and you have probably used reversed polarity a few times without knowing. Europe, excluding France, has plugs that are designed to be plugged in either way around, thus it is irrelevant which way live and neutral are wired. French domestic plug sockets have a three-pin system. French plugs look virtually the same as the European plug but the earth is connected via the hole in the plug. You do not need to worry about this as long as your mini extension plug has earth-bonding straps on the outside as well as an earth hole for France.

Designed for France and Europe. Note the earth hole between the silver pins and the earth bonding strap at the bottom.

People intending to Offsite-Park long-term may consider fitting a solar panel. Motorhomers we have spoken to say their solar panels are able to maintain the battery at full charge during lay-up, but not when they are occupying the motorhome. The reality is you will be able to park offsite for longer, but you will not have enough power to watch TV every night. If your motorhome is stored somewhere without hook-up, then the viability of fitting a solar panel increases and may offset the hundreds of pounds needed to buy a solar panel system. The Achilles heel of solar panels is they barely produce any power on inclement winter days when power is most needed by the occupants. There are different types and makes of solar panels and without individually testing them you cannot know their true performance, so do your research before you part with your cash. A solar panel fixed to the roof of

Solar Solutions fitting a solar panel at a motorhome show.

Solar panels need an air gap to keep cool.

a motorhome will not perform as well as advertised because the intensity of light will only be good when the sun is high in the sky. Ideally, you want a moveable panel, either portable or rotating on the roof, so you can aim it toward the sun. Motorised, computer-controlled panels can track the sun, but are very expensive. The 75W solar panel seen in the photo below had been in service since 2006.

The owner explained that it only worked in sunshine, though modern panels can work in overcast conditions. The photo was taken on the 30th of August at midday in sunny conditions and the panel was generating 4.6A of 12V electricity. The owner said that he had a solar panel fitted flat on the roof of his previous motorhome and he estimated that he would need 200W worth of roof-mounted panels to achieve the same output he was getting from his current 75W setup. He also said that 200W worth of panels would cost nearly as much as one motorised panel.

75W sun tracking solar panel on a Dutch motorhome parked at a stellplatz alongside the Mösel River.

Small wind turbine.

Wind turbines have similar issues to solar panels and can run in conjunction with them, but you may become a slave to electricity generation. Wind turbines start working at five knots/5.8mph and realistically will only trickle charge a battery until the wind is strong, but who wants to camp in a windy place? The biggest problem is securely fixing them. Pegging them out on the ground is difficult and contravenes the rules of setting up camp when you are entitled only to stop at the side of the road. Some people fix turbines to the rear of their motorhomes but complain they are noisy at night. When not in use where are you going to store it? And how easy is it to erect?

Generators will recharge your on-board batteries and enable you to watch endless TV, as well as charge your electric bike or mobility scooters' batteries. American motorhomes often have large generators fitted as standard so that air-conditioning can be run. European manufacturers' may offer generators on the options list for some top of the range models. The reality is that few people use a generator, or at least they are rarely seen in use, because there are so few places where a responsible tourist can run one. Unsurprisingly generator use is rarely allowed at campsites. Placing a portable generator on the ground is illegal at Motorhome Stopovers or when Offsite-Parking. In addition, storage and weight for both the generator and fuel is likely to be a problem. Thankfully there is a quiet and practical generator available as long as you have £3,000 to spend. The Self Energy EG 20 is a LPG fuelled generator that produces 20A. These units are chassis-mounted and probably will not be noticed by when running during the day. The whole thing weighs 19kg and there is no additional fuel weight as they use the gas from the gas cylinders.

Self Energy EG 20. Photo: Conrad Anderson.

SUPERCHARGER 50 AMP.
Photo: Ian Hamilton Cooper.

Good quality portable generators are relatively inexpensive and they command good second-hand prices. Nevertheless before you go shopping use your motorhome for a year to see if you actually need extra power. Cheap generators are available, but as always you get what you pay for, and a noisy, whiney and smoky 2-stroke generator will soon upset people around you. Even the best petrol generators are noisy in a quiet location and the reverberation will irritate people around you whenever you use one, therefore the less they are run the better. According to the manufacturer, The Supercharger 50 amp portable generator delivers a charge rate of 50A per hour. This is achieved by utilising an automotive alternator powered by a four-stroke petrol/LPG engine. See www.thesupercharger.co.uk.

Fuel cells have the potential to provide sufficient electricity for most motorhomers. Efoy fuel cells run on highly flammable methanol and this has limited availability but 10L will be enough for weeks or possibly months, see www.efoy.com. These units are light, economical and virtually silent, but you may find it hard to justify

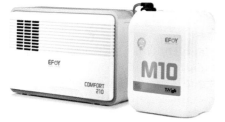

Efoy fuel cell and methanol fuel © SFC Energy AG.

spending £2,500 for 3.3A of electricity generation. People with a very big budget could have a Truma VeGA LPG powered fuel cell fitted. They are compact, run on LPG and can produce 6,000W per hour at 20A. See www.conrad-anderson.co.uk for more information about the fuel cells from Efoy and Truma as well as the Self Energy EG 20.

LED lights use between 5 to 10 times less power than tungsten filament bulbs. LED lights come in various shades of white, yellow or green, so be sure you can try them and return if unsuitable. See www.ledbulbs4u.co.uk.

Electricity has inherent dangers. Mains electricity has sufficient energy to cause a fatality, and a 12V short circuit could start a fire. We do not condone unsafe practices, nor is the previous an installation manual. We merely make general comments. When considering carrying out any maintenance, repairs or installations seek professional advice. All leisure vehicles, as part of their annual service, should have the electrical systems inspected by a qualified electrician. Second-hand vehicles without supporting documentation should also have their electrical systems checked; if in doubt seek professional advice.

Go Motorhoming and Campervanning

Gas

Appliances that run on gas within the motorhome typically include the fridge, hob, and oven. Most motorhomes have a space efficient, combination blown-air heater and water heater hidden in a locker. Some motorhomes have a wall-mounted gas powered

Cooking toast on gas is easy, simply dry fry bread in a pan.

convector space heater and separate water heater. Gas is extremely flammable and can be explosive. Correct safety procedures need to be followed and regular servicing undertaken by a qualified person is advised.

There are two gasses used in motorhomes, butane and propane, both are types of liquefied petroleum gas (LPG). All the appliances will work on either gas without adjustment, and the most important difference is operating temperature. Butane will not change from its liquid state to gas below 0.5°C, whereas propane can be used in temperatures as low as -42°C. Butane is also denser than propane. Calor Gas 7kg blue butane cylinders and 6kg orange propane cylinders have the same dimensions. The same is true for the 13kg and 15kg cylinders, respectively.

There is no EU-wide agreement for gas cylinder connections. Even in the UK different connectors are required for cylinders of competing brands.

Left, German exchange gas 11kg cylinder, right a refillable cylinder.

The result is that the cylinder connections vary widely and different regulators or hose tails will be required depending where you buy a new cylinder. There is some interchange but the easiest way is to buy the appropriate regulator or hose tail with the cylinder. Calor Gas is the market-leading brand in the UK, but there is no exchange or refill agreement outside of the UK for this or any other UK brand. Campingaz is sold in numerous

European countries, but it is impractical to use due to its small 2.75kg size. Since 2003 all EU-built motorhomes and caravans operate their gas systems at 30mb, early German models operated at 50mb. Gaslow sells a range of adaptors for most European cylinders.

Most British motorhome gas lockers are designed to accommodate two 6/7kg Calor Gas cylinders. Most continental motorhomes accommodate two 11kg cylinders, which is a

Spanish Euro fitting and pump.

common size, but a 6/7kg and a 13/15kg Calor Gas cylinder will normally fit. If you intend to visit only one country, especially if you intend to visit the same country year after year, purchasing a foreign cylinder and appropriate attachment/regulator is cost effective and sensible.

So that an exchange can be planned, you need to know how much gas is in your cylinder. The definitive way to find out how much gas is left is to weigh the cylinder, German cylinders have weights down the side and

Big flame caused by water from the washing up draining into the burner.

Calor Gas cylinders mark the empty weight (curiously in pounds) on the aluminium collar. Externally fitted gas pressure gauges will read full until all the liquid has been turned to gas. Automatic changeover units are nice to have but far from a necessity and could leave you with no reserve. We have only used our reserve cylinder when topping up our refillable cylinder.

The LPG that is used instead of petrol and sold at fuel stations may be a mixture of butane and propane and is suitable for motorhome gas systems. Motorhomes can have a fixed LPG gas tank fitted just like a car, and these tanks have an 80 per cent cutoff valve for safety. Filling beyond this point increases the risk of liquid propane/butane passing through the regulator. Liquid on the wrong side of the

Truma Ultraheat gas and 230V convector heater fitted in an Adria Coral Compact.

regulator is potentially catastrophic because the liquid expands approximately 250 times as it turns into a gas, and the pressure is likely to cause a gas leak or significantly increased flame. With the correct adaptors it is possible to refill gas cylinders but they must not be filled beyond 80 per cent because it is dangerous to do so. This rules out filling Calor or any other European exchange gas cylinders. Only gas cylinders that are fitted with 80 per cent cut-off valves are designed to be refilled by the general

The Cup	Denmark	**De-Visser (also known as the Bayonet)**	**Acme**	Slovakia
France	Greece	United Kingdom	Belgium	Switzerland
Italy	Hungary	The Netherlands	Germany	
Portugal	Turkey	Norway	Ireland	
Austria	Croatia		Luxembourg	
Switzerland	Sweden		Poland	

public. You can buy refillable gas cylinders from Gaslow at www.gaslow.co.uk, Tel: 0845 4000600, and Autogas 2000 who supply lightweight aluminium cylinders, visit www.autogas.co.uk, Tel: 01845 523 213. Refillable gas cylinders eliminate rental cylinder exchange problems and adaptor/hose tail incompatibility. Filling up with LPG from fuel stations is much cheaper than exchanging a Calor Gas cylinder. When you come to sell your motorhome simply keep your refillable or sell it separately. Refillable cylinders fitted with a float gauge rather than a pressure gauge are preferable, but the secret is to refill before the gas level becomes low, they can be topped up at any point.

> *The gas from two 11kg gas cylinders was all that was required during six months wintering in the United Kingdom from September to February. Campsite showers, a laundry and electric hook-up were used. The caravan's water heater and fridge ran on electricity, and an electric fan heater and kettle were used.*
>
> *During a one-month ski tour in temperatures ranging from 0°C to 21°C, without electric hook up, we used the gas from one 11kg cylinder per week. In these temperatures a refillable cylinder and a spare cylinder is the most convenient.*
>
> *Our Cityvan was fitted with an under-worktop Thetford fridge-freezer. This worked extremely well but used the gas from one 11kg cylinder per pitched week during the summer.*

LPG Availability

There should be no problem filling a fixed tank abroad but a refillable gas cylinder may be refused especially if it is taken out of the motorhome locker. We recommend that you fit an external filler point for your refillable cylinders to prevent any problems. In our experience if you are turned away at one fuel station the next will probably welcome your trade, but it helps if you have the correct filling attachment connected before you get to the fuel station. The three main filling adapters are shown in the picture opposite.

LPG is difficult to obtain in parts of Europe. LPG availability is detailed in the *All The Aires* guides and online at www.go-motorhoming.co.uk. Country specific websites include: http://stations.gpl.online.fr (France), www.volvo200.org (Sweden), and www.gjelstenli.no/lpg (Norway).

Safety

Gas is highly flammable. Gas cylinders should always be turned off in transit unless a Truma Drive Safe Gas Regulator is fitted. Vents in the well of the gas locker must never be covered or blocked with mud or snow. Gas cylinders must be transported and used in a secure upright position as liquid butane/propane could pass through the regulator resulting in a very big flame. Suspected gas leaks should always be investigated fully using soapy water before appliances are used. Gas leaks on ferries are potentially catastrophic, as gas sinks to the lowest point creating a potentially explosive atmosphere. Therefore gas systems should be turned off before embarkation. All leisure vehicles, as part of their annual service, should have the systems inspected by a qualified LPG engineer.

Water Systems

Motorhomes can have three separate systems: fresh water, dirty water from sinks and showers called wastewater/grey water and toilet waste also called black wastewater.

Motorhomes generally have a fixed freshwater tank, normally located internally, smaller Van Conversions often have one or two refillable plastic canisters. A secure internal fresh tank is preferable when Offsite-Parking and essential in sustained freezing conditions. A tank that holds less than 100L is insufficient when Offsite-Parking. On campsites, it is nice to have a water tank that does not need filling daily, but fully serviced pitches that provide constant fresh water are becoming more common.

Water is heavy, one litre weighing one kilo and to stay within the motorhome's weight limits it may be necessary to discard fresh water before departing. This is fine if you know exactly where you are going, but inadvisable if you don't. It is sensible to keep enough for a night, in case water is not available when you arrive or you are late.

Two 12L water bottles fitted in Concept Multi Car Reimo Van Conversion.

On average, two adults experienced in Offsite-Parking use 20L of water per day for drinks, washing up and other essentials. Showering uses up to 15L per person, possibly more if long hair is washed. 5L is plenty for a strip wash. Washing clothes uses 20L of water. With strict water conservation it is possible to use less than 20L a day, but far easier to use more than 100L. Four nights is the longest we have stopped away from a water supply and we still had 30L left in our 110L tank.

Always ask if water is available wherever you stop and when gathering Offsite-Parking information from other motorhomers. People using Motorhome Stopovers and

Drinking water at Ediger Burg Stellplatz alongside Mösel River, Germany.

Offsite-Parking on an 'as we find them' basis generally travel with water tanks at least three quarters full, so it is possible to stay a few days. Many experienced Offsite-Parking motorhomers carry a full tank of water and 20L containers of water at the expense of other items.

There are several ways to fill motorhome water tanks. Motorhomes with internal or under-slung water tanks normally have an outside filler point, which looks similar to a fuel cap. Many campsites and Motorhome Stopovers have areas designed for motorhomes to discharge and restock with water. A short length of food-quality hose is useful but you will need various tap connections. Water tanks located under seats or between floor layers usually have a large inspection/filler hole making filling easy. We almost exclusively fill up the tank through the inspection/filler hole and use a 20L plastic water bottle to transport the water from the tap. Plastic watering cans are popular for keeping tanks topped up. Whatever you intend to use, ensure it is food quality as plastic items, especially hoses, can cause a chemical taste similar to the antiseptic TCP.

Water quality varies across Europe and can appear a little dubious, even when marked 'potable'. Bottled drinking water is cheap and widely available from shops but costly on space, weight, and convenience. Drinking water is available in campsites and some town squares, hopefully marked 'potable', sometimes identified by seeing people filling drinking bottles. Water may have a cloudy appearance or a chemical

CAK waste trap and Nature Pure water filter.

taste. Water purification tablets or liquids can be used if you have concerns about water-borne bacteria. A water filter is most convenient and they are relatively easy to fit. Some water filters are designed to improve clarity, smell, and taste, but you actually need to install a water filter that eliminates bacteria as well as nasty tastes. Replacement filter cartridges may need to be carried if you intend to travel more than six months.

As discussed in the gas section, a gas powered water heater is likely to be fitted inside a cupboard. 10-15L of hot water is heated in about half an hour. Depending on the model an electric element may be fitted, but it is unlikely to be cost effective to retro fit one except for people that regularly winter in their motorhomes. Boiling a kettle and using the shower block is cost effective.

Truma combination water heater fitted in our Cityvan.

Summer campers can make use of a solar shower. This is a black plastic sack with a shower head coming off it. Basically you fill it with water and leave it out in the sun all day to heat up. On very hot days the water can get too hot and cold water will need to be added before use. Please remember when Offsite-Parking and using Motorhome Stopovers it is illegal to set up camp.

Wastewater, commonly called grey water, refers to dirty water from sinks and showers. Wastewater is either collected in a fixed tank mounted under the floor or an outside portable container. Motorhomers wishing to Offsite-Park or use Motorhome Stopovers must have a motorhome with a fixed tank. It is common practice for a fixed wastewater tank to be 10 per cent smaller than the freshwater tank. One of the few disadvantages of motorhome use is when pitched on campsites, it is inconvenient to pack up and move just to empty waste tanks. You can use an empty toilet cassette for transporting wastewater. Curiously, wastewater leaves a smell that cannot be rinsed away. Campsite staff and subsequent campers get upset if they find a pile of food waste that inevitably collects when wastewater is drained on pitch. Campsites that do not have a motorhome Service Point sometimes have a drain cover that can be lifted, but it is best to ask upon arrival.

Benicassim motorhome Service Point in Spain.

Chris emptying a toilet tank at Dudelange Aire, Luxembourg.

Disposing of wastewater is easy at a motorhome Service Point, but carry a short length of hose to direct the water directly to the drain. Draining your waste tanks anywhere other than at an official place is likely to be illegal and harmful to the environment because of the chemicals and surfactants. Some motorhome manufacturers seem unaware that it is essential that waste tanks completely drain to prevent an unpleasant smell building up. Snail-trails of wastewater are commonly seen on roads near motorhome Service Points, and this is likely to upset local residents. People intentionally leave drain taps open and it may be necessary to go up and down steep hills and round tight bends to completely empty the tank. Tank smells are inevitable during hot weather, but you can reduce this by restricting the volume of bacteria friendly liquids such as oils, starchy water, and washing up water. Pouring diluted bicarbonate of soda occasionally down the drains helps to keep the tank clean and reduces smells; proprietary products are available. You could fit a waste trap to the drainage pipe under the sink and an example can be seen in the water filter picture on page 82. External tank contents will freeze in sustained freezing conditions. See Wintering in Chapter 4.

Toilet waste, commonly called black water, must be disposed of responsibly as it poses a health risk. Emptying toilet cassettes into public toilets is generally unacceptable because it is almost impossible to empty a toilet cassette into a toilet without making a mess. Furthermore, it is probably illegal and will almost certainly upset local residents.

Motorhomes such as American RVs with fixed toilet waste tanks have to be driven to the Service Point unless on a suitably serviced pitch. When plumbed into an on-pitch waste system the tank must still be used and emptied periodically. Leaving the drain valve open will result in a build up of solids in the tank. Attempting to use a bucket to empty a fixed toilet tank, will almost certainly cause an agricultural outcome, and is definitely antisocial for neighbours. Most Motorhome Stopovers have a waste drain but access may be a problem.

RV draining toilet then wastewater at Calais.

There are several variations on how toilets flush. Our least favourite automatically flushes when you open the waste hole and it may be necessary to turn off the water pump in certain situations. Some toilets have a flushing reservoir and toilet flush chemical can be added, but the tanks are prone to growing algae, which then sticks to the bowl when the flush is activated. Some toilet flush systems are directly fed from the onboard water supply. This is a curious arrangement as water bylaws state, in domestic and industrial situations, that fresh water systems must not be able to siphon contaminated water. Household toilets have a cistern to ensure that drinking water cannot become contaminated. We strongly recommend that you make up a spray bottle of toilet flush solution and spray both the toilet bowl and flush exit every time you use the toilet.

Potty training is a necessary subject. When you want a number two there are some things you must do. Wet the bowl by flush or spray and place toilet paper around the exit hole. If you keep the hole open during proceedings, and you have good aim the bowl will stay clean. It is worth scrunching up some toilet paper and dropping it down the hole first to reduce the risk of splashing.

Remotely located campsites often have septic tank waste systems. Toilet, 'blue', chemicals often contain biocides, which effectively kill the bacteria that make the septic tank function. Using environmentally friendly 'green' chemicals or a SOG system are suitable alternatives. SOG is a brand name for a simple extraction system designed for built-in cassette style toilets. These extraction systems are more efficient at controlling toileting smells than proprietary chemicals, as a constant airflow is drawn through the toilet bowl. This is very welcome in a small space especially when sharing the motorhome with less than intimate friends. This system is relatively easy to fit if you have basic 12V electrical knowledge and have the arms of a contortionist. A SOG system is definitely good value for money and we consider these essential. This ultimate environmentally friendly system cuts out the weight, space, cost, and need of chemical. Concentrated blue chemical also stains everything it comes in

SOG toilet extractor fan being fitted at a show.

contact with. The only negative of a SOG is vented smells may be directed to your neighbours or 'worse still' into your awning. Chimney systems are available, visit www.soguk.co.uk, Tel: 0845 8698940.

When touring, discharge wastewater and toilet waste at every opportunity, regardless of tank levels, as your next stop may not have facilities. Some campsites charge you for servicing if you only stay one night, so always read the small print.

All motorhomers represent the motorhoming community. Offsite-Parking motorhomers need to be particularly responsible, especially when it comes to disposing of toilet waste. Dumping a toilet full of chemicals and waste in the countryside is environmentally unfriendly, unnecessary and probably against the law everywhere. It is not always possible to dispose of waste as regularly as you would like. The following options all have their merits.

Two toilet cassettes: Carrying a spare toilet cassette in an outside locker is favoured by German motorhomers. Cassettes are relatively expensive, bulky and weigh about 20kg when full. Fiamma produce a Porta Kassett designed to carry a spare toilet cassette underneath the motorhome.

By limiting the toilet to urine only, not even toilet paper, will increase the time before emptying, also the emptying experience is less hideous. We also use this technique when on campsites simply because of the emptying experience. Public toilets or the bag technique (see text in blue) can be used to deal with solid waste.

Toilet emptying and water collection at Ouistreham Aire, France.

Warning! The following text in blue contains the realities some people will not want to know, so if you are not going to Offsite-Park move onto Chapter 4.

The bottle technique: Men can refill lidded bottles and discard the waste in a bin or down a toilet when available. Plastic fabric conditioner bottles with wide necks are worth saving.

The bag technique: Use bags for your solid waste including toilet tissue. Incidentally, bags specially designed to hold in place in Thetford toilet bowls are available in German camping shops. Carrier bags work well, but always check for holes! We recommend having a pee before attempting this procedure and advise that toilet paper is put in the bag, just in case. Disposal in communal wheelie bins, that are commonly available all over Europe, ensures waste is safely disposed of as these bins are also used for nappies and sanitary wear. When immediate disposal is not possible the bag can be stored in an airtight jar; sauerkraut jars are particularly suitable. Some people have not worked out responsible toileting and disappear into the bushes with a roll of toilet paper, charming!

Vicarious Books

One Stop Motorhome and Caravan Bookshop

All the Aires

- Aires inspected and photographed.
- GPS coordinates taken onsite.
- Aires for large motorhomes identified.
- Best Aires guides for: France; Mountains; Spain & Portugal; Belgium, Holland & Luxembourg.

ACSI Camping Card

There are other low season discount schemes but none rival the quantity and freedom of this no commitment guide. Buy the book, it's as simple as that and camp across Europe for a maximum of €16 a night. The card presses out of the cover.

Sea View Camping

This unique campsite guide shows you all the sea view campsites around Great Britain. All you have to do is choose where you want to go and be ready for a fantastic time as you explore one of the most diverse coastlines in the world.

France Passion / España Discovery

Like a glass of wine? Then why not spend a night at the vineyard where you can see, smell and taste the process. Other guides for Italy and Germany.

Camping Morocco

With 100 open all year campsites and 50 off site parking places, Camping Morocco is ideal for winter sun or summer fun.

Stopover Guides for all of Europe

We specialise in importing stopover guides from Europe: Reise Mobil Bord Atlas for Germany, Camper Life for Italy, and Camperstop Europe for a general guide across Europe.

Campsite Guides for all of Europe

We also stock the superb ACSI DVD, Caravan Club's guides to France, and Rest of Europe, Alan Rogers and a range of other guides.

0131 208 3333   www.Vicarious-Shop.com

CHAPTER 4 - Preparing Your Motorhome

There are more gadgets and gismos available than you can poke a proverbial stick at. The reality is that many motorhomes do not have the payload for unnecessary items and you may have to sacrifice one must-have gadget for another.

Essential Items

Items you must carry in your motorhome to comply with the various laws of European countries include: a first aid kit, fire extinguisher, red warning triangle (two in some countries), spare bulb and fuse kits, spare wheel or repair kit, EEC labelled reflective vest for each passenger and two pairs of driving glasses if you need them.

Bare Necessities	
Legal	**Administration**
2 red warning triangles	Driving licences
Fire extinguisher	Insurance and vehicle documents
First aid kit	Money and cards
Headlight modifiers	Passports (visas)
Reflective vests	**Safety And Security**
Spare bulb and fuse kits	Smoke alarm
Spare wheel or repair kit	Carbon monoxide alarm
Two pairs of driving glasses	Safe

Some people put their reflective vests over the seat backs. This is a good idea because in some countries you are legally required to wear them when you exit the vehicle on the roadside. The country initials where the vehicle is registered must be displayed when driving on the continent. Euro number plates display the country initials within a blue box on the left-hand side and are accepted within the EU. You must display a national decal when travelling outside of the EU. Right-Hand-Drive headlight set-ups must not dazzle oncoming drivers. Applying headlight modifiers is easy, but to do it successfully you need to be able to see the beam pattern. Shining the headlights onto a wall at night is best. You need to flatten the pattern by eliminating the kick ups on the left-hand sides. We recommend that you carry at least one spare set of headlight modifiers in case of loss or damage.

Security

Crime involving motorhomes is low but you can greatly reduce the risks by not stopping at motorway services, day or night. Crime hotspots include the main routes through southern France and Spain. Thieves also target unattended vehicles in supermarket car parks. Criminals like easy targets, therefore physical security devices make the motorhome less attractive. Integrated alarms, immobilisers, and trackers provide peace of mind and may attract discounts off insurance fees. The following data was provided by Thatcham Research in May 2013. 'Depending on where you live in the UK and which vehicle you drive, the chances of getting your vehicle recovered are low and decreasing, given that a large amount of vehicle theft is now attributed to international, organised gangs who will very quickly aim to get your vehicle out of the country and most likely strip it for

parts. However, if you have a Thatcham Category 6 stolen vehicle tracking system fitted the chances of recovery increase to 65-70%. With a Category 5 system which automatically tracks unauthorised movement of your vehicle and alerts the relevant authorities your chances of recovery rise to around 99%.'

Campsites may seem like safe havens, but petty theft is common especially at campsites near capital cities. We recommend that you be as vigilant at campsites as you would when Offsite-Parking. Always lock up when you leave your motorhome unattended, even for just a minute whilst you pop to the loo. Thieves usually choose the easiest option and physical security not only slows down an attempted break in or theft, it also makes a statement to opportunist criminals. To find out the vulnerable parts of your motorhome, pretend to lock your keys inside and ask friends, especially agile teenagers, to 'break in' with you without causing damage. Safety and security items are often sold on fear, and supporting literature and sales patter often highlights the worst-case scenario. Ask for data from independent companies before parting with your cash.

This Autocruse has a double locking system but often only one latch is located at the centre of the door.

The following points highlight the most important areas of weakness to address. The caravan (habitation area) door is the most likely place for a thief to try and force open, so additional locks are essential. Exterior opening lockers are also vulnerable. Locks are available in several styles from strong deadlocks to lockable grab handles. Fiamma and Milenco produce deadlocks, though their design makes it possible to be locked out and in. Cab doors can be held shut by passing a ratchet strap through the handles, it may also be possible to secure doors with the seatbelts. Fitting a steering wheel lock is sensible. Sliding window security is improved by cutting a dowel to fit into the bottom channel, thereby jamming the window. Covering fixed ladders prevents easy access to vulnerable skylights. Outside sensor lights are convenient for you and could disturb a potential thief or make you aware that something has come close to the motorhome. Audible sensors are also available.

Immobilisers have been mandatory on new vehicles since 1998 and most ignition systems now require the correctly coded key to start the engine. This has made hotwiring a vehicle a thing of the past and most vehicles are stolen using the original keys, thus key security is even more important. Immobilisers fitted post-sale also prevent the engine from starting and may be integrated into an alarm system. Often an electronic key fob is used to arm and disarm the system. If you attach this to your keys and they are stolen, the security advantage is lost. Some immobilisers utilise a Radio Frequency Device (RFD), which allows the engine to start as long as the device is inside the vehicle. Often the RFD is credit card-sized therefore convenient to carry in a wallet or purse.

Put the seatbelt through the door handle to hold the door shut, also note the steering lock.

www.uk-towbars.net custom build strong storage boxes.

Alarms sounding are so common that most people ignore them, therefore unmonitored alarms are only useful if you are within earshot. Some alarm systems send messages to data centres, who in turn contact named persons, should an event occur that requires attention. Other alarm systems send messages to personal telephones to notify the recipient of a given event. In our opinion, this level of contact is necessary as we previously had an unmonitored alarm that regularly went off without our knowing.

Our Cobra Alarm was unintentionally set off at least once a day when the key fob is carried in a pocket.

Alarm systems designed for motorhomes monitor the doors and lockers and have an internal movement sensor. The most reassuring feature is the perimeter alarm and this is something we use at night both on and off campsites. When you select the perimeter setting the internal sensor is not activated, so people and pets are able to move around inside, whilst the doors and lockers are monitored. Always check the alarm key fob carefully before committing to an alarm as bad design can lead to frustration when the 'panic' alarm is constantly triggered from your pocket.

Vehicle trackers should reduce the time taken by police to recover a stolen vehicle. Hopefully the criminals will be caught and any insurance claim settled quicker. Cars stolen by professionals in the UK are more likely to be stripped into parts rather than resold, and the first five hours from initial theft are critical for recovery. Trackers operate in different ways and provide varying levels of service. Trackers can be self-installed for less than the cost of a one-year subscription for a branded product. These inexpensive trackers are self-monitored via a mobile phone SIM card; they even offer the option to cut the fuel supply.

Choosing the correct alarm or tracker is complicated and thorough research will be necessary. Ensure that there is an adequate level of service across Europe and confirm who liaises with the local police. Purchasing a system that has been tested by an independent body should prevent you from making a bad purchase. There are two key UK companies, Thatcham and Sold Secure. The Motor Insurance Repair Research Centre, known as Thatcham, rates alarms, immobilisers and trackers in categories from 1-7 and a full list of approved devices with appropriate contact details is available on their website www.thatcham.org, Tel: 01635 868855. The device may also have been tested by Sold Secure. A searchable database of approved products is available on their website www.soldsecure.com, Tel: 01327 264687.

Alarms and trackers can be fitted by most motorhome dealers and by alarm and tracker specialists. We are currently testing an Out Smart the Thief system that is fitted to our Aventura see www.606060.com. Additional security can be purchased at motorhome dealers, motorhome shows and online.

Every year Vicarious Books receives two or three phone calls from customers who have had their motorhomes broken into. The common theme is that no additional physical security was in use and that the valuable items taken were not secured in a safe. Often just a briefcase or bag has been taken, sometimes all the cupboards have been rifled. The simple rule is, if you do not want to lose it, do not take it with you. Important documents have to be taken with you and should be stored securely. No system is foolproof and delaying a determined thief or negating an opportunist situation is probably the most you can achieve. Small, reasonably light safes are available from DIY superstores and Argos. It is hard to get a good fixing in a motorhome so choose a safe that you can fit into the floor well or a cupboard. Laptop safes with enough space for all essentials are worth considering.

Security does not finish with physical deterrents, common sense or simple tricks of the mind are is just as important. A good example is sticking multi language labels on windows explaining that a sophisticated alarm is fitted.

Every time you park consider the following:
• Parking in a visible and illuminated space rather than an isolated dark corner.
• Keeping your valuables out of sight, preferably in a safe.
• When you go to bed leave a 'muggers wallet' out on the side so your real one is not searched for (see page 166).
• Tie a dog lead on your bike rack or leave a pair of size 12 gents' shoes under the step.
• When you go out shut the curtains and blinds and leave a light or radio on so that people assume the motorhome is occupied.
• Never leave keys lying around or on display at any time.

Safety

Smoke alarms designed for caravans are less prone to going off when you burn the toast and often have a temporary silence function. They cost around £20 and it would be silly not to have one. Likewise, a carbon monoxide alarm should be considered essential. Carbon monoxide is an odourless, colourless, and tasteless gas, which is produced when burning fossil fuels, such as LPG, ineffectively. Initially carbon monoxide is undetectable to humans and mild levels will cause early symptoms of poisoning like lightheadedness, confusion, headaches, vertigo, and flu-like effects. When the concentration is above 100 parts per million it is highly toxic if enough is inhaled. Motorhomes generally have gas cookers, heating and hot water systems, which can potentially produce carbon monoxide. Ensure that the annual habitation service engineer tests these items sufficiently. Each time you go away in your motorhome test that the smoke and carbon monoxide alarms are

This alarm displays the actual level of carbon monoxide but others have an audible alarm only.

Following repairs our fridge leaked exhaust gasses containing carbon monoxide into the motorhome. This was easily fixed by securing the top baffle.

working. Kidde produce an inexpensive combination carbon monoxide and smoke alarm.

Gas alarms are devices that detect LPG gas leaks and the anaesthetic gasses alleged to be used in burglaries. Gas alarms have sold very well due to the fear of 'Gas Attacks', and this is a good thing because a gas leak from the LPG system is infinitely more likely than criminals trying to render occupants of vehicles unconscious by spraying in highly flammable gasses. Gas attacks are reportedly happening at motorway service areas when vehicles are broken into. The Royal College of Anaesthetists released the following statement in 2007, and confirmed they still stand by the statement in 2013:

'It is the view of the College [of Anaesthetists] that it would not be possible to render someone unconscious by blowing ether, chloroform or any of the currently used volatile anaesthetic agents, through the window of a motor-home without their knowledge, even if they were sleeping at the time. Ether is an extremely pungent agent and a relatively weak anaesthetic by modern standards and has a very irritant affect on the air passages, causing coughing and sometimes vomiting. It takes some time to reach unconsciousness, even if given by direct application to the face on a cloth, and the concentration needed by some sort of spray administered directly into a room would be enormous. The smell hangs around for days and would be obvious to anyone the next day. Even the more powerful modern volatile agents would need to be delivered in tanker loads of carrier gas by a large compressor...

The other important point to remember is that general anaesthetics are potentially very dangerous, which is why they are only administered in the UK by doctors who have undergone many years of postgraduate training in the subject and who remain with the unconscious patient throughout the anaesthetic...

If there was a totally safe, odourless, potent, cheap anaesthetic agent available to thieves for this purpose it is likely the medical profession would know about it and be investigating its use in anaesthetic practice.'...

We have spoken to 12 couples that have had their motorhomes broken into whilst stopping at motorway rest areas. Some of the people woke up, others could not believe they could sleep through a robbery and two couples assumed they must have been gassed. It is a strange thing that people often sleep through domestic burglary yet no one assumes they have been gassed. The reality is that motorway service stations and parking areas are busy, noisy, transient places and the thieves are professional. To our knowledge no victims that believe they were gassed have been blood tested to prove that anaesthetic was inhaled, nor have there been any reported deaths or reports of motorhomes exploding because they were filled with highly-flammable anaesthetic gas. If you have bona fide evidence to the contrary, please let us know.

Remember that everything we do in life involves an element of risk. The best way to avoid the risk of burglary is simply to never stop overnight at motorway service or rest areas, instead stay at a local campsite or Motorhome Stopover. Do not drive until you are too exhausted to make sensible decisions. Plan long drives with an hour break every four hours and do not drive for more than eight hours per day. When travelling with children reduce driving times and take more breaks. Whenever you park somewhere where you feel there is a risk of crime, set your motorhome's alarm, keep doors and windows shut and locked and valuables secured in a safe.

Driving Safety And Comfort

On average UK Coachbuilt motorhomes travel 3700 miles per year. However the tyres are capable of covering 40,000+ miles and it is very common to see the original tyres on quite old motorhomes. The compounds that tyres are made of naturally degrade with age, especially when exposed to strong sunlight, and tyres over five years old may well need replacing irrespective of tread depth. Make a routine inspection of your tyres each time you go away in your motorhome, check the overall condition, tread depth, look for cracking, and check the tyre pressures. Since motorhomes are always fully laden, tyre pressures need to be higher than you might expect or even higher than that advised by the chassis manufacturer. The motorhome handbook should display the correct tyre pressures, if there is any doubt contact the motorhome manufacturer. This photo taken in

The cracking on this nine-year-old tyre leaves no doubt that it should be replaced.

April 2010 shows the number, 1501, printed on the sidewall of a tyre fitted to a motorhome that was for sale. 1501 identifies the manufacture date to be week 15 year 2001. Some people cover the tyres to protect them from the sun and this may be worth doing when parked up for a long time. It is important to change the resting position of the tyres and we recommend that you drive the motorhome fortnightly to keep the engine lubricated and guarantee a new resting point for the tyres.

Michelin, Pirelli, and Continental tyre manufacturers have designed tyres specifically for heavily laden motorhomes, the main feature being extra sidewall reinforcement. They are often referred to as camping tyres, but are correctly identified by the letters CP, standard van tyres are marked with a C. New motorhomes not built upon motorhome specific chassis often have C classification tyres fitted. We have used "camping tyres" manufactured by Michelin, Pirelli and Vanco Continental. All performed well in wet and dry conditions, gripping to the road under heavy braking and when driving faster than most motorhome users would on mountain roads. Overall we prefer Michelin Camping Tyres. If you are likely to encounter snow on your trip, consider fitting mud and snow tyres which are designed to provide more grip in icy conditions. Mud and snow tyres are identified by one of the following symbols, 'M+S', a mountain or a snowflake.

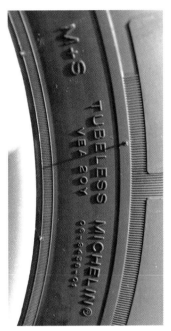

Winter tyres are often marked M+S.

A reversing camera system should be high on your wish list and should be selected when you are filling out a sales order for a new motorhome. You are most likely to damage your motorhome when manoeuvring at very slow speeds and any visual advantage you can give yourself is worth having. Little dents and scrapes on motorhome bodywork are expensive to repair and may require the whole panel to be replaced to do a proper job. The armed forces train their logistics personnel on how to give and to react to reversing commands. Military drivers are trained not to look in their mirrors when receiving directions from a banksman who remains at the front of the vehicle during the entire reverse manoeuvre. We have never seen this done by motorhome couples, but have seen plenty of comical situations with communication breakdown. We recommend that you agree your manoeuvre communication signals then take your motorhome to a large empty car park or field and practice common manoeuvring situations. Reversing camera systems can automatically switch on when reverse gear is selected. Whilst driving, they can be used to view trailers or traffic behind you. When parked, they can be used as a security device enabling you to see and hear what is happening outside. The monitor can also double as a TV. Ensure that the reversing camera is positioned so that you can reach it from the ground because the lens needs regular cleaning in wet conditions and they also suffer from condensation. You will become reliant upon your reversing camera, though you will not realise how much unless it breaks down.

Suspension enhancement is not necessary on a well-designed and correctly loaded motorhome. Fitting air suspension aids to motorhomes significantly improves ride comfort when they are very wide, tall or have large overhangs and should prevent the feeling of a boat at sea. Ensure that load and brake-monitoring systems will not be affected before fitting because altering the ride height could cause any load-sensing device to provide unbalanced front and rear braking. Whether it is worth adding suspension aids is purely down to cost against use during ownership, and should not be an excuse for overloading. For further information visit www.airide.co.uk, Tel: 01202 489771, also visit www.as-airsuspension.co.uk, Tel: 01925 740666.

Get Lost

When we were Full-Timing our outlook was "How can you get lost when you don't know where you are going?" Oh how things change. Now that we have entered the satellite age, you might think that maps are pointless. The reality is maps are as important as ever because motorhoming is as much about the journey as the destination. If you blindly follow your satellite navigator, you will drive along main roads and motorways, missing scenic routes or sites of interest that you could have seen along the way. Like most people we use a satellite navigator when we are driving on unfamiliar roads, but unless we are driving alone, the sound is muted and the satellite navigator is used only as an aid alongside map navigation.

Advance route planning allows you to study your maps and consider your preferred routes. Maps normally detail scenic routes, thermal waters, viewpoints and places of interest, many of which will not be found in

Always look before commiting to a turning that your satallite navigator recommends.

guidebooks. You cannot rely on buying good maps as you enter a country, so investigate and purchase all the maps you need before you leave the UK. Vicarious Books stocks popular European maps and Stanfords London shop has a big range of maps that are also available online at www.stanfords.co.uk, Tel: 020 78361321. Strange as it may seem, European maps can be written in English and we once drove past Wien in Austria when we fully intended to visit Vienna as printed on our map, we still have not been to Wien (Vienna). You need to be able to navigate minor roads, so you need maps at a scale no more than 1:400,000. Europe-wide road atlases do not go down to this scale, so you will need to buy country specific maps. Road atlases are easiest to use when in transit and fold out maps are good for route planning. A Europe wide map is essential when information sharing with other motorhomers. Write the information you gather directly onto the map, that way you will come across it if you decide to travel in that area or country again.

There are many satellite navigation machines available and, until now, we have usually said you get what you pay for, but this is one time where it appears not to be necessary to spend a lot of money. A handheld satellite navigator can be used when away from your motorhome and this is an enormous advantage compared to a fixed installation. Over the past five years, we have tested and used five different models and brands of satellite navigator and can confirm that they all navigated us to our destination most of the time, although sometimes they get lost. They all tried to navigate us down unmade tracks and sometimes did not have roads that have clearly been there for decades. All suggested farcical routes such as driving many miles in the wrong direction to a motorway junction when we were already on a perfectly good road travelling in the correct direction. 'Satnaff special shortcuts' are our favourite, some are so crazy you ask yourself who programs these things? That said, we consider a satellite navigator an essential item and carry two just in case one breaks down. We rely heavily on our satellite navigator in large towns when we are trying to find somewhere in a backstreet, and they come into their own when used in conjunction with accurate GPS Coordinates. Nearly all the destination guides sold by Vicarious Books have GPS coordinates for each place listed and for that reason, we strongly recommend you buy a satellite navigator.

There are two ways to program a satellite navigator to locate a specified place, either type in an address or a coordinate. Typing in postcodes works well in the UK because they are street specific, but in Europe postcodes cover a large area, often a whole town and its surroundings. When you want to pinpoint an exact location you need a coordinate; to complicate this there are three commonly used coordinate types:

- Degrees, Minutes & Seconds, written as: N51°04'53.88' E001°10'58.92'
- Degree Decimal Minutes, written as: N51°04.898' E1°10.982'
- Decimal Degrees, written as: N51.081639° E1.183031°

Guidebooks may use any one of the above types of coordinate, for example Vicarious Books uses the Degree Decimal Minutes format (N51°04.898' E001°10.982'). Be aware that not all Satellite Navigators accept coordinates, and those that do may only accept one type.

The Prime Meridian runs through Greenwich, London and measures 0°. Meridians are measured up to 180° east or west of the Prime Meridian and represent longitude on the globe. The equator, at 0°, represents the centre of the earth from the north and south poles and the latitudinal lines known as parallels are measured up to 90° north and south of the equator. In order to pinpoint a position, each set of coordinates, no matter which type, has two parts. Each part is a collection of numbers and symbols behind a letter; either N or S depending if you are north or south of the equator, and E or W depending whether you are east or west of the Prime Meridian line. If no letters are displayed then west is indicated as a negative figure i.e. -10.1234°.

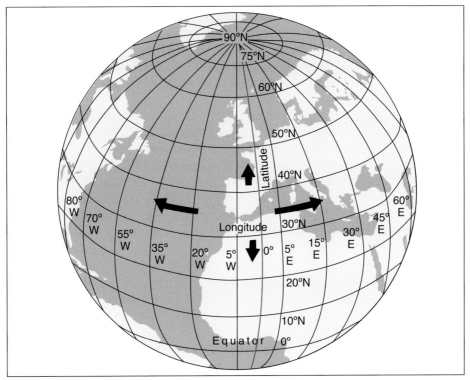

Meridians and parallels – the basis of measuring time, distance and direction.

Ken Rowley explains how to covert the different types of coordinates:

Decimal Degrees are usually given to four or five decimal places. For example four places of a decimal number i.e. 10.<u>1234</u> has an accuracy of 36.4 feet. Five places of a decimal number i.e. 10.<u>12345</u>, improves the accuracy to 3.64 feet, just less than 3'8". Degree Decimal Minutes are often given to three decimal places i.e. 10°<u>12.345</u>' this gives an accuracy of just over 6 feet, close enough to be acceptable for our needs.

The maths needed to change between the formats is not complicated and can be readily achieved using a basic calculator. The compass direction at the beginning of each coordinate does not change. The degrees value does not change; this is the number between the compass direction (N, S, E, or W) and the first punctuation, either a degrees symbol or a full stop. For clarification the underlined text on the following coordinates stays the same: <u>N10°</u>12.345', <u>N10.</u>12345°, <u>N10°</u>12'20.7'.

Changing Degree Decimal Minutes into Decimal Degrees. *To convert N10°12.345 ignore for now the degrees value (see above) and divide the minutes, everything after the degree symbol, by 60. In the example N10°12.345 minutes, 12.345 is divided by 60 = 0.20575. Add the degrees value and directional letter, N10°, to the front of the .20575 and the answer is N10.20575°*

Changing Decimal Degrees into Degree Decimal Minutes. *To convert N10.12345°, ignore the degrees value (see above) and consider the decimal part of the degrees, everything past the full stop, N10.12345. Multiply 0.12345 by 60 = 7.407'. The number to the left of the decimal point (which may be one or two digits) represents the minutes, while the decimal number to the right of the decimal point .407 shows the decimal minutes, add the degrees value and directional letter and the conversion is N10°7.407' minutes.*

To avoid possible confusion minutes are always specified by two digits before the decimal point. This means that 7.407' minutes is written (and entered into your satellite navigator) as 07.407' so the answer above is correctly given in the form N10°07.407'

Degree Decimal Minutes into Degrees, Minutes and Seconds. *To convert N10°12.345' simply multiply the seconds, which is the very last part of the coordinate N10°12.345' by 60. Ignore the N10°12 and multiply .345 by 60 = 20.7. The 20.7 is added to the end of the N10°12 to make N10°12'20.7'.To convert Degrees, Minutes and Seconds into Degree Decimal Minutes simply divide the 20.7' by 60.*

Both parts of the coordinate must be converted and it is imperative the correct letter is assigned to each part and take care to put the decimal point in the correct place. However, when choosing a satellite navigator I would strongly recommend that you buy one that takes all three coordinate types. It makes life much simpler!

When you buy your satellite navigator, ensure you find out where you input the GPS coordinates and which types it can take. Do not take a sales representative's word that the machine accepts coordinates. We recommend that you test the three different types of coordinates to make sure the satellite navigator identifies the correct location, the following coordinates all relate to Vicarious Books shop on Tontine Street in Folkestone: N51.081639° E001.183031° or N51°04'53.88' E001°10'58.92' or N51°04.898' E001°10.982'. You must enter every symbol when you enter the coordinates. Both TomTom and Garmin produce some satellite navigators that accept all three types of coordinates.

Satellite navigators are easy to use as long as you read the handbook, even technophobes should cope. The satellite navigator will be set to its default settings when you take it out of the box and you may wish to change some settings to suit your preferences. Often you can choose to avoid toll roads, choose the shortest route, the fastest route or main routes. If you select 'fastest route' the satellite navigator will select country lanes with a national speed limit of 60mph over main routes restricted to 40mph. If you select 'shortest route' the routes are likely to include narrow country lanes and we have been directed to drive off-road down green lanes. No doubt, programmers will address these issues in time.

Before you drive off blindly following your satellite navigators' instructions select your destination and preview the chosen route. You may have to input some 'via points' at strategic junctions if you want to make the satellite navigator choose specific roads. When you are under way and the satellite navigator directs you to turn off always assess the road before turning into it and be prepared to turn around if necessary. We strongly recommend that you update your mapping every year. This is best done online so that the satellite navigator's software can be updated at the same time, you may need help with this. Give yourself plenty of time as it takes a long time to download and upload the mapping.

Some satellite navigators are pre-programmed with bridge heights and weight restrictions and we recommend that you confirm which countries are covered. Having entered the dimensions and weight of your vehicle, the satellite navigator should avoid routes with bridges that are too low, or roads with unsuitable weight and width restrictions. It is our opinion that this feature is unnecessary for motorhomes not exceeding 3m tall and less than 3,500kg. Remember, it is essential that the satellite navigator takes all three types of coordinates. Garmin sells the Dezl as a large vehicle satellite navigator.

Basic Kit

Motorhome manufacturers wishing to pass type approval follow the guideline in British Standard European Norm (BSEN) 1646-2 4.4 Personal Effects to ensure that enough weight is allocated for luggage, cooking and camping equipment.

Go Motorhoming and Campervanning

The Standard provides manufacturers with the following weight calculation: 10x the number of berths, plus, 10x the length in metres. This is easier to understand as 10kg per bed space and 10kg per linear metre. This equates to 110kg for a four berth, 7m motorhome and is supposed to be enough weight for four people's chattels. Our basic everyday equipment used by two people weighs 240kg. This is not surprising when you take into account, shoes, bedding, food, drinks, kitchen, bathroom, and camping equipment, tools, oils, and lubricants. Other items that are commonly carried but not included in the 240kg include bicycles, hobby equipment, laptop, camera, books, TV and satellite system. Each belted passenger seat has 75kg allocated (excluding driver). Therefore, a four-berth motorhome with three belted passenger seats has 225kg allowance for passenger weight. This is in addition to the Personal Effects allowance. Everyone is advised to weigh their loaded motorhome including the intended passengers, luggage and chattels, and full fuel and water tanks. See Chapter 2 to understand maximum weights and payload. In the unlikely event that you have any spare weight capacity you can consider adding the extras from your wish list. We strongly recommend that you make an inventory that includes the individual weights of each item carried.

Campernalia

Campernalia is an international multi-million pound industry, providing a multitude of items for your every whim, from self-heating food to kitchen sinks. None of these is essential but some are worth considering.

Awnings

Awnings can be used only at campsites or other areas where camping is permissible. If you predominantly intend to use Motorhome Stopovers or park offsite then there is no point buying an awning. There are two types of awning that you can use at campsites.

A wind-out awning is a fixed, roof height roller blind that can be set up in a minute. This

Wind-out awnings should only be used where camping is permissable.

Free-standing awning.

provides useful shade that also keeps the sun's heat off one side of the motorhome and a dry area during light showers. Side panels are available for further comfort. This type of awning can be broken in windy conditions and awnings attached to the side of motorhomes are easily damaged when driving in confined areas. A removable awning blind is the budget choice, but takes more effort to set up on site.

Free-standing awnings are ideal for campsite-based motorhomers pitching for a week or more at a time. This type of awning often resembles a tent and is self-supporting, so can be left on pitch when the motorhome is taken offsite. In transit they are bulky, taking up valuable storage space and payload.

On The Level

Parking on level ground is an unusual luxury, whether at a campsite or at a Motorhome Stopover. When you are pitched at a campsite you can use levelling blocks, often referred to as chocks. The law forbids the use of levelling blocks when you are parking in a Motorhome Stopover or Offsite-Parking, so you will have to choose a parking area and

Bigger levelling blocks required on this campsite pitch!

make do. Some motorhomes come with steadies; these are legs that can be wound to the ground to stop the motorhome rocking when stationary.

These are far from necessary and the effort of placing them down, and their weight, can negate their benefit. Once again these must not be used at Motorhome Stopovers or when Offsite-Parking. Over time you will find that the motorhome is so rarely level that you might not notice.

Cab Window Screens

The cab windows provide very little thermal protection. Screens provide additional insulation, in both extremely hot and very cold weather, and provide privacy if there are no curtains or interior concertina windscreen blinds. There are two types of screen available, internal and external. External screens fit over the outside of the motorhome, which

Internal screens being used in a Motorhome at Stopover Dol de Bretagne.

means they can get wet and dirty, needing to be dried, and cleaned, before storing. Internal screens get wet when in use as they inevitably touch the cab windows, which suffer condensation as soon as outside temperatures

External screens should not be used at Aires.

fall and inside humidity levels reach 60 per cent. Only internal screens can be used when Offsite-Parking or using Motorhome Stopovers. Another option is to retro fit Remis concertina blinds to the framework around the window. Although expensive, they can be opened and closed in seconds and can provide adequate insulation when closed.

Mosquitoes is the one intruder that are guaranteed to join you in your motorhome. To keep them out every window and vent should be fitted with a secure fly-screen. This material is widely available and can be retrofitted if necessary. The door also needs protection and we found that a Fiamma Moskito Net proved effective even in Finland where mosquitoes are prolific.

Air Conditioning/Cooling

Southern Europe is hot enough in August to justify the use of an air conditioning or cooling system, otherwise these are unnecessary. Before handing over a large amount of money, consider the power consumption and supply, as most air conditioners require a 230V electricity supply and even if they do not they will drain your leisure battery quickly. Also consider the effects of the weight of the unit on the roof, the wind resistance, additional height and the cost to run and service it. A cheap and simple alternative to air conditioning is a 12V fan fitted in a top vent, Fiamma and Omni Vent both produce models that work well and it is also worth fitting a top vent all weather cover. Top vent fans are sometimes standard equipment on new motorhomes and should be selected if on the options list. They can also be retro fitted, although wiring the 12V fan may prove challenging if there is no light close by to take a feed from. The fans fit into the common size top vents and can be switched to extract or blow air into the motorhome. Being reasonably quiet and as low as 0.5A these are great as cooking/condensation extractors. When 230V is available you can use a fan or an oscillating fan heater, with the heater elements turned off, to create a breeze.

Additional Modes Of Transport

Motorhome Stopovers located in towns and villages tend to be within walking distance from the shops, restaurants and sites of interest. Campsites are usually located out of town and an additional mode of transport or public transport is required to get around.

Bicycles are the most popular additional mode of transport amongst motorhomers, mostly because they are the only practical option. Cycling is an excellent way of occupying yourself and keeping fit. Before you fit a bike rack, consider whether you will actually ride the bikes that have been collecting dust in your garage for years. Copenhagen and Stockholm are ideal cities to explore by bike

Bicycles are the most practical form of additional transport.

and many other European towns have bicycle routes. The best cycling countries are Belgium, Holland, Germany, Denmark and Hungary. Most national parks have cycle routes to explore and some have mountain bike routes. Spares and repairs are easy to get all over Europe and bikes are available to hire in many places. There are three types of bicycle to consider. If you only want to

Electric bicyles are practical transport.

cycle gently to the shops or around site then a folding bike is perfect. If you want to make more of your bike, consider a hybrid bike that is a cross between a mountain and road bike. It should have at least 10 gears. Couples with different cycling abilities could consider a tandem as the stronger cyclist will help the weaker and will not be constantly waiting. The Cycle Tourer website, www.cycletourer.co.uk, details cycling across Europe. Also worth checking are www.nationalcyclenetwork.org.uk and the European Cycling Federation www.ecf.com.

Cycle racks are light and relatively unobtrusive, although bikes get dirty no matter how well you cover them. The Fiamma Carry Bike can hold up to 60kg, a standard bike weighs around 14kg, and an electric bike weighs 28kg (including battery pack but not charger). Displaying a red and white striped hazard square to a rear protrusion is a legal requirement in some

Another practical transport option or perhaps a hobby trike.

countries. These hazard signs are available from accessory shops at home and abroad. If your motorhome has a garage or large lockers consider storing your bikes inside. The motorhome's rear axle loading or available payload may dictate whether or not you can take bikes with you, see Chapter 2. Ensure your travel insurance covers bicycle related accidents.

Some motorhomes will not have sufficient weight capacities to carry a motorbike.

Scooters or motorbikes may seem like the ideal transport when the motorhome is parked onsite. Unfortunately, few motorhomes, even those with garages, are legally capable of carrying the additional weight of a scooter once passengers and chattels are loaded, thus a trailer is necessary. Scooters weigh about 100kg and a scooter rack weighs at least 70kg. See Chapter 2 to understand payload and rear axle loadings.

We see more British registered motorhomes towing cars than we do from all the other countries of Europe put together. We put this down to a lack of knowledge of continental motorhome facilities. First-time continental motorhome buyers will have seen motorhomes parked offsite and at official Motorhome Stopovers and may have a Motorhome Stopover in their town or village. In contrast, UK first-time buyers may not even know about Motorhome Stopovers or understand that it is normal not to stop at campsites. If you feel you need a car, we recommend that you buy a caravan, as explained in Chapter 1.

There are two different ways to tow a car, the undisputed legal way is to load it on to a trailer and the other option is an A-frame system. The A-frame system is a convenient and simple solution once the car is adapted. A simple frame is attached to the front of the car, which enables the car to be hitched to the motorhome like any other trailer. Although this system is not illegal in this country, as long as trailer rules are complied with, this may bring unnecessary police attention to you in countries where it is unusual. Most people will not be able to reverse when an A-framed car is attached to the motorhome. In 2005 the Department of Transport released a fact

An A-frame towing system.

sheet entitled 'Note on A-Frames and Dollies' stating '...*we believe the use of "A" frames to tow cars behind other vehicles is legal provided the braking and lighting requirements are met. However, while this is our understanding of the meaning of the Regulations, it is only the Courts which can reach a definitive interpretation of the law.*' People requiring further information should contact PRO-Tow Frames, manufacturers of CAR-A-TOW, visit www.caratow.com or phone 01202 632456.

Fitting a tow bar reduces the motorhome payload by at least 30kg. Licence holders restricted to towing 750kg will have to purchase a micro car or take a further driving test. Micro cars weighing less than 750kg MAM are built by Axiam (www.axiam.com), Microcar (www.micro-car.co.uk), Ligier and DUÉ (www.ligier.es).

This specialist trailer is available in France from www.labissonnette.fr

Please remember that it is not reasonable to take up excessive space on a Motorhome Stopover because of your trailer, and some Motorhome Stopovers now ban trailers. Unhitching your trailer when Offsite-Parking or on a Motorhome Stopover is just the sort of thing that upsets local residents and causes restrictions to be applied. Campsites often charge extra for towed cars and trailers.

Entertainment

Television And Radio

Tuning into the BBC's World Service when abroad will be easier if you have the frequencies list published by the BBC. The BBC World Service is broadcast via satellite all over Europe from Hotbird 9. Dozens of radio stations are broadcast on satellite TV and on the internet, which enables you to listen to your favourite UK radio programmes.

Television is one of those things that seem to contradict the essence of motorhoming. Nevertheless, you will be glad of the entertainment on rainy days or long winter evenings. Keeping up with the action can prove extremely beneficial when you are following a major sporting event like the Tour de France. Make sure your television and aerial are digital compatible because Europe and the UK are currently engaged in a digital switchover. European countries sometimes broadcast programmes in English, often films, and you are likely to get the gist of the weather forecast in any language. Televisions powered by both 12V and 230V are preferable so that an inverter is not required. Modern flat screen monitors are easy to store and some motorhomes come with TV mounting brackets or cupboards. If you don't want to take a television, you can still watch a film on a laptop with a DVD drive or a portable in-car DVD player.

Portable Computers

Portable computers can entertain you in so many ways and they are economical on 12V. Modern laptops have vast memories and additional storage drives are inexpensive so you can store unlimited music, maps, tourist information, language courses, audio and text books. Also you can play games and watch films on DVDs or listen to CDs and they are great for viewing and storing digital photos. If you dream of writing a book, now might be a good time to start. Try writing a weekly or monthly blog and publish it free on a website such as www.blogger.com.

Consider securing your laptop in a laptop safe or by attaching a lock known as a Kensington Lock. Laptops have a small hole that can accept a Kensington Lock and a wire hawser is looped around a secure object in the motorhome, such as a seat, making it hard for thieves to grab the laptop and run off.

Laptops can be secured with a Kensington lock.

Using a satellite system is the only guaranteed way to receive English television programmes if you travel outside of the UK and Ireland. Depending on your location, you will be able to receive many of the channels you tune into on digital TV at home. Satellite television provides welcome entertainment on wet days and you can watch as much as you like if you have a 230V electricity supply. You can watch about ten hours of TV when you are relying on one 110Ah leisure battery, then you will need to drive for several hours or hook-up to electricity to recharge the battery.

Many European motorhomes have a folding satellite dish.

Satellite System Components:

Satellite dish

Coaxial

Satellite decoder box

Scart or HDMI lead

TV

Tuner and compass

Satellite television systems are easy to operate and tune in. First, find an area where you can aim the satellite dish at the broadcasting satellite without any obstructions such as trees. Use a compass and satellite finder to find the exact direction. The parabolic reflector (dish) collects the signal and reflects it back to the LNB. The LNB is the device on the end of the arm which collects the concentrated signal before sending it down the coaxial to the satellite receiver box. The bigger the dish the stronger the signal reflected back to the LNB. The satellite receiver box then translates the signal and sends it via a scart or HDMI lead to the television.

With the exception of Sky, most UK channels are broadcast 'Free to Air'. Sky digibox users should read their terms and conditions before installing the satellite receiver in their motorhome. Freesat is another UK provider and Freesat receivers will display channels selected by that operator. Free to Air compatible satellite receivers can lock into signals from broadcasters all over Europe and most British channels are available. Buying a Free to Air receiver is a logical choice and there are 12V and 230V models.

Most people fix the satellite dish to the motorhome roof, but trees and other obstructions are inevitable wherever you park and a few leaves is enough to block the signal. This is bad luck when you are Offsite-Parking, but campsite users can set up a dish some way from their pitch as long as it does not cause inconvenience to others. You only have to walk around a Spanish campsite to see that TV reception is a conundrum for all nations and large 1.2m dishes are a common sight.

All you need to watch TV in southern Spain is a massive dish and a lucky break in the trees.

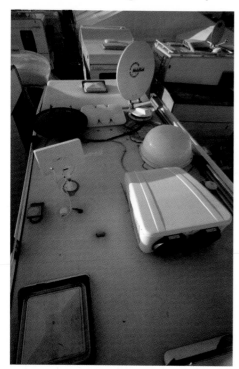

RoadPro's motorhome has van-aerial disease, due to frequent tests.

Satellites broadcast English channels over the UK and some areas of Europe and the intentionally covered area is described as a satellite footprint. The signals spill over to the middle of Norway, southern Greece, Sicily, southern Spain, and eastern Europe and that is why some people use a 1.2m dish. The problem with a 1.2m wide dish is storage when in transit. To get around this some people fix their dish to the rear ladder.

Good reception is all about preparation, even if you have a self-seeking dish. You will have to walk or drive around a campsite before you reserve your pitch to ensure there is one without signal-blocking obstructions. Bad weather weakens satellite signals and you may have to wait for it to pass before you can lock in to the satellite signal. Once the satellite decoder is locked in, it may lose signal during heavy rain or snow and strong wind may move the dish. Onlookers often muse at motorhomes jigging around their pitch performing the 'dance of the satellite' for the sake of satellite reception.

When setting up manually adjusted dishes, first adjust the elevation. In Norway, the dish is nearly straight up and down, and in Sicily, the dish will nearly collect water. Then adjust the LNB skew (polarisation) left or right. RoadPro has a PDF on their website under 'Tech Tips' that provides the angles. Finally aim the dish to the east and adjust the satellite finder so it is not squeaking and no lights are on. Now turn the dish slowly to the right; it will pass over some weak signals. When it reaches 28.2 mil east on the military scale compass or 158° on a standard compass, depending on which you prefer to use, the finder will go off the scale. Turn the finder down to fine tune. Fine tuning can also be done up and down if necessary. After a few seconds delay the signal strength and a lock indicator should come up on screen, this can take a while on the outskirts of the footprint.

Satellite TV is an evolving medium, so please make further enquiries before purchasing a system. www.satelliteforcaravans.co.uk has detailed information on different types of satellite televisions, receiver boxes, and dish sizes for use in Europe. RoadPro sells satellite systems and provides detailed and useful information in their catalogue, visit www.roadpro.co.uk, Tel: 01327 312233. Also see www.viewersguide.co.uk.

Hobbies

Planning your trips around your hobbies will help to structure your time if you do your research in advance. Be sure you know which are the best places at different times of year and ensure you have the equipment you need with you.

Campers enjoying a boules game.

Bulky equipment may need special storage such as a roof or bike rack-box. Beware these boxes can become the motorhome equivalent of a loft, and roof boxes create significant drag, so only fit when space is limited and spare payload is available. Arts and crafts make excellent motorhome hobbies as they are very time consuming and the equipment is often lightweight. Needlepoint, crochet, tapestry, and knitting are ideal and you may be able to sell your creations to other

Gather your walking infomation before you depart.

campers or present them to your friends and family upon your return. You are never short of something to draw, either from life or a post card. Even if you have never drawn before there are a range of books to get you started. Photography is an excellent hobby, not only can you record your travels you could even sell your photos online. Search 'stock photos' for potential outlets and read the requirements. Why not share your experiences with your friends by uploading photos on social media sites like Facebook, or onto your personal photo gallery or blog.

Our motto is 'If in doubt, leave it behind', but we have also found that on the day that we wanted to go swimming, walking or fishing we did not know where to go so make sure you have the relevant information with you.

Arabba Motorhome Stopover. Photo: Andy Glasgow.

Preparing Your Motorhome For A Winter Trip

First, remove all unnecessary items from the motorhome: summer chairs and tables, windbreaks, lanterns, flags, buckets and spades, BBQ, wetsuits, and summer clothes. Then load snow chains, a shovel, gloves, kneeling mat, water storage bottles (filled), hot water bottles, electric heater, hand brush, broom, cardboard/carpet, extra bedding, insulating screens, generator and fuel, tow rope/wire, winter clothes and shoes/boots. Now weigh your motorhome and see if there is any payload left for you, your luggage and food.

Ensuring your motorhome is in good working order is essential before embarking on a trip up the mountains. If you are in any doubt about the condition of your vehicle get it serviced or checked by a mechanic.

Tyres

Ensuring your vehicle has the correct tyres is the most important element of preparation if you want the best chance of staying on the road in icy conditions. We looked at the tyres fitted on a cross-section of UK motorhomes and campervans whilst preparing this guide, and discovered that 95 per cent are not fitted with winter tyres. Tyres with an M&S (mud and snow), snowflake, or snow-capped mountains image are winter rated tyres. Michelin M+S camper tyres perform extremely well in winter mountain conditions.

Winter tyre requirements vary from country to country. In Austria, from November to April, winter rated tyres or tyres marked M+S with a minimum tread depth of 4mm must be fitted. Snow chains are compulsory where signs indicate. Germany requires visitors to fit winter tyres and on-the-spot fines are issued to ill-prepared drivers that become stuck or impede the flow of traffic, so snow chains must be fitted when there is a covering of snow or ice. In France snow chains must be fitted on snow-covered roads when indicated by signs. In general, every country will expect winter visitors to be equipped to drive safely in snow, failure to do so could result in a fine.

Mountain routes may be impassable at any time between November and March. In northern Scandinavia, road closures due to snow are common until the end of May.

Snow Chains

Snow chains fitted to the vehicle's driving wheels makes driving possible even in the iciest of conditions and it is advisable to carry snow chains in Andorra, Austria, France, Germany, Italy, and Switzerland. It is important to follow the Highway Code for each country and always follow chain manufacturer's instructions. Snow chains should only be fitted when the roads are completely covered in snow or ice.

Snow chains. Photos: Andy Glasgow.

Fitting snow chains for the first time is equivalent in difficulty to learning to ride a bike, so practice fitting and refitting them in warm, dry conditions until you can fit them without thinking about it. Wear tough but thin work gloves, fitting chains is fiddly and thick leather gloves are useless. To assist in clearing snow around tyres it is worth carrying a stiff brush, a folding shovel, and a kneeling mat. Once fitted, drive 4-5m and then retighten the chains, periodically stop and check chains whilst driving. Should you ever hear a repetitive cloncking noise whilst driving with chains, stop immediately as a broken section of chain may be flailing around the inside of your wheel arch. Repair links are often supplied with chain sets for a temporary fix, and a bungee will replace the elastic should it be necessary and can help to tighten the chains evenly. To prevent your chains from breaking: keep your speed down (in Germany the max speed is 50kph), avoid harsh acceleration/braking, spinning wheels, and driving on asphalt. Also take care mounting levelling blocks and do not drive over the connectors when removing chains. Untangled chains stored between sheets of newspaper will be ready for next time.

When making parking choices consider your exit, and avoid parking down a slope. If snow is forecast, fit your chains before going to bed or out for the day.

Engine Condition And Fuel

Before embarking on a trip to the mountains it is important to ensure your vehicle is in good running order. Tired, older vehicles may struggle with the gradients, lower oxygen levels at altitudes, and the cold. The vehicle's brakes should be checked to ensure they are in good condition before you undertake miles of steep descents.

In very cold conditions diesel solidifies into a waxy gel if antifreeze is not included. Depending when and where you buy diesel you may also

Photo: Andy Glasgow.

need to buy and add special antifreeze to your fuel tank. From early November, all fuel stations in Austria change over to winter diesel rated to -20°C. If you buy fuel in southern Spain or Sicily, then climb to the top of the respective mountains, park overnight and wake up to -10°C or below, you won't be going anywhere until the diesel warms up. Diesel pumps at mountain fuel stations usually identify that the fuel is treated.

When outside temperatures fall and rise quickly, particularly overnight, atmospheric moisture condenses into water droplets on the inside of the fuel tank, above the fuel level. Truckers and farmers habitually fuel up their tanks at the end of the day to prevent this happening. Water is heavier than diesel and readily separates if the two are mixed together. Fuel filters catch water and slowly fill from the bottom up over time; this water can freeze thus preventing the engine from starting or running. In freezing conditions regularly drain off the fuel filter. Simply unscrew the drain tap located at the bottom of the filter a couple of turns until diesel replaces water. You will need a receptacle to catch the water/diesel.

The only way you can be sure that there is enough antifreeze in your engine coolant system is to measure it with a hydrometer, these cost as little as £5. The ethylene glycol level needs to be between 40-50 per cent to withstand potential temperatures as low as -25°C. Also, ensure your screen wash is concentrated enough to cope with the cold. Check your vehicle handbook to confirm whether low-viscosity, cold-temperature oil is required for your engine. Your engine battery must be in good condition, if in doubt take it to a garage to be tested.

Life In The Freezer, Preparing Your Utilities

Most modern motorhomes will be perfectly suitable for taking on a skiing holiday; although they are not known to be good skiers, they will provide warm and comfortable accommodation. The three utilities: gas, electricity and water need managing to ensure a comfortable trip. Make sure that your motorhome has recently had an annual habitation service and that the gas systems were serviced, not just visually inspected. Also, ensure that your carbon monoxide detector and smoke alarm are working.

What A Gas

Gas is essential for heating and cooking in your motorhome. Expect to consume one 11kg gas cylinder per week when not plugged into mains

Local gas cylinders available at fuel stations in France.

hook-up. Many people have invested in refillable gas cylinders, but if you have two, leave one at home, as you are going to have to use pure propane below 0°C and LPG Autogas across Europe nearly always has some butane mixed in. Butane remains liquid below 0.5°C, propane turns to gas as low as -42°C. In freezing temperatures the propane in your refillable cylinder is able to evaporate leaving the butane as a liquid. Each time you fill up the percentage of butane in the refillable increases. To get around this problem use the refillable during warm days when the butane can evaporate, and buy a local propane cylinder to use at night or when below freezing, remember to pack the appropriate pigtails.

Simple gas convector heaters, commonly fitted in caravans, are unfortunately rare in new motorhomes, apparently because of travel noise complaints. Their advantage over blown-air combi boilers is that they consume no 12V electricity in operation unless a supplementary blown-air system is used, an important point as heating may be required 24hrs whether occupied or not. If you are lucky enough to have a convector heater and it has a roof flue, ensure an extension pipe is fitted, thus preventing snow from burying the flue vent.

Go Motorhoming and Campervanning

Metered mains propane gas is available at some Austrian campsites; its use may be cost effective if you plan to stop a long time. A flexible hose connects to your regulator. Gas is supplied at 50mb, but your regulator will compensate.

Austrian mains gas. Photo: Andy Glasgow.

Electricity

Most new motorhomes will have a 12V, power-hungry, blown air heating system, and the unit will consume most of the available leisure battery supply, an 110Ah in good condition will provide power for 24-48hrs. It states in the Truma manual that a Combi 6 will use 5.6A at start up and 1.3A on average but you will be in colder than average temperatures so will use more than 1.3A. Solar panels will provide

Electricity available from a pre-pay meter.

an insignificant amount of extra power and wind turbines could be a blowout. If you wish to visit a resort for more than 24 hours the only reliable way to provide enough power is to plug into mains electricity or run a generator or a fuel cell. There are plenty of open campsites and Motorhome Stopovers, with electricity, around the ski resorts. The electric hook-up charge may be more than usual, but it will be used all day and night to keep your motorhome warm and dry, so value for money is not an issue. Campsites near ski slopes often have drying rooms and warm shower blocks. Small ski resorts may not have campsites, but Offsite-Parking may be tolerated at the Gondola car park. When Offsite-Parking a generator will be a necessity but cheap 2-stroke generators are unpopular as the high pitched running noise and smelly fumes will soon annoy your neighbours. 4-stroke generators are quieter and very popular.

Photo: Andy Glasgow.

Water And Servicing

Visit a Service Point before ascending the mountains. It is common for water to be off or frozen at Motorhome Stopovers. Do not turn off water taps found running as the warmth in the water stops them freezing. Always fill up in the afternoon as taps are often frozen in the morning. Water and waste stored in under-slung tanks is prone to freezing. Insulation helps but the only way to

Leave taps as you find them.

ensure the water stays liquid is to fit a heater element. Many people also carry drinking water in plastic containers inside the motorhome. Ensure you secure them in transit and that they do not leak. This may be your only fresh water supply if your tank freezes.

To prevent your water system and liquid goods from freezing you have to run heating constantly, possibly on the lowest setting during the day whilst out. If you run a blown air system with ducts running through lockers, these should prevent any problems. Simple convector heaters, gas or electric, will not prevent pipes located in the depths of lockers from freezing. When researching *All the Aires Mountains,* the Glasgow's found their water pump and drop valve suffered first, but keeping cupboard and internal locker doors open helped. Electric fan heaters can blow warm air into cold/damp spots, defrost frozen windscreens and other frozen areas like engines for example. Parking with the sun on the side of the motorhome that contains the water pipes is a great help.

Most modern motorhomes have a built-in frost safety valve near to the water-heater. This valve opens automatically when the temperature gets close to freezing point and allows the water stored in the boiler to drain. If a pressure-sensing water pump is on then all the water in the system will drain. Truma set their frost valves at 7°C, this safety feature is very useful if you have laid up your motorhome for the winter, but not so useful if you are using it in cold conditions. The valve is unlikely to trip when the boiler is in use. Be aware that, when on electric hook-up and using secondary electric heating, the water-boiler cupboard will need heating. It states in the Truma manual that you can run the heater before you fill the boiler with water, thus bringing the temperature above 7°C. An optional 0.4A heating element is available for the frost valve.

Keeping the wastewater tank tap open and draining water into a container is good practice, but any residual wastewater is still prone to freezing. Water expands by nine per cent when frozen so do not fill your wastewater tank and reduce the amount of water entering it. Use as many on-site facilities as possible and wash-up in a bucket or bowl and dispose of the water at the on-site disposal point. The larger the amount of frozen water in your wastewater tank, the longer it will take to defrost.

Before leaving your motorhome unused in cold weather, all liquids must be drained off (waste, fresh water and toilet waste) including all pipework as much as possible. Remember to drain your water-heater, toilet-flush, sink-drain-traps, and remove your water filter. Opening all drain valves and taps then drive up and down steep hills to empty pipes. Remove all liquids and foods stored in cupboards that could spoil or burst if frozen.

Insulating Your Motorhome

Insulating screens are essential as the cab glass offers the least insulation of the whole caravan conversion. The cab itself offers the second least insulated area and curtains that isolate the cab area are worth retrofitting. We believe that on balance, internal screens are preferable to

Photo: Andy Glasgow.

externally fitted screens, despite offering less insulation. The condensation that forms on the windscreen often needs defrosting then quickly removing with a squeegee. Van Comfort has a good range of screens, see www.vancomfort.co.uk.

Condensation occurs when airborne moisture condenses on a surface that is colder than room temperature. Removing your window screens in cold conditions demonstrates this instantly. The best way to control condensation is good ventilation but this makes the occupants cold. Motorhomes are reasonably airtight apart from the intentional and essential vents so do not block them with the exception of fitting the winter fridge covers. Vans converted to campervans can suffer draughts from the rear and sliding doors, and may not have enough insulation.

Use a squeegee to remove condensation.

Cooking and showering produce high levels of moisture. Gas releases one litre of water for every litre burnt, so avoid long cooking sessions. Always cook with lids on pans and keep a top vent open, run extractors if fitted, turn the heating up to compensate as this also helps to expel the steam. Keep up the regime whilst eating and until the washing-up is dried up. Shower with the top vent ajar, use blown air heating if available and squeegee the walls dry as soon as possible. Use the bathroom as your airing cupboard for damp clothes and towels and keep the top vent ajar and heating vent open. Fan heaters help to keep the air moving thus preventing some condensation build-up. When driving between sites run the cab heating fans on full. Should you be lucky enough to get too hot, open a rear window or top vent to create a through draught.

In really cold weather you may need to insulate every window. All you need is bubble wrap, double-sided sticky tape, scissors and some attachable suction pads. These items are available from most DIY stores in Europe. Simply tape two or more layers of bubble wrap together and cut to the right size for your window. Windows with roller blinds will hold the bubble wrap in place. Use suction pads to hold the bubble wrap in place on cab windows. We have tested these home-made screens down to -18°C and found they helped considerably.

Go Motorhoming and Campervanning

A second layer of carpet, or plastic runner, on the floor offers extra insulation, takes the wear and tear, and can be discarded at the end of the season. We also lay cardboard above the carpet to absorb the inevitable water that comes in each time you enter the motorhome. We recommend you lay cardboard before border posts to protect the carpet from the wet, and often muddy, boots of the customs officials.

Bedding

To keep warm in the cold we use a four-duvet system in winter; it sounds over the top but works well. Typical 5" foam mattresses or cushions do not offer enough comfort or insulation so one covered duvet is used as a mattress topper/sheet and all duvets are laid on the bed. Then

Andy Glasgow loves sleeping in his Luton.

depending on how cold it is you can choose to sleep under one, two or three duvets. Place hot water bottles in beds one hour before retiring. Choose bottles with thick fluffy covers, as they stay warm all night. Hooded tops are ideal for sleeping in when it is really cold. Andy and Sue Glasgow, who researched *All the Aires Mountains* by Vicarious Books, love their luton over-cab bed as they find it the warmest place to be. The top tip is do not let yourself get cold before going to bed, as it takes ages to warm up and it stops you from sleeping.

Poor bladder control may not be the culprit of bed wetting in very cold conditions. Moisture constantly evaporates from our skin, and beds suffer a build up during prolonged use. When the base of the bed is cold, moisture naturally condenses where the mattress touches it. This is a real problem on beds without slats but a coir underlay mat, www.drymesh.co.uk, helps to keep the air moving. Make a conscious effort to air the mattress or cushions daily, simply propping them up should be enough.

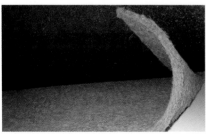

Coir matting helps airflow under the bed. Photo: Andy Glasgow.

Snow On The Roof

The title is not intended as a euphemism, more a warning. Snow is known as a good insulator but thawing and refreezing could create your very own rooftop glacier, so sweep off fresh snow as soon and as best as you can, pressure washers may help remove ice on roofs.

Photo: Andy Glasgow.

Take great care on the roof of your motorhome in winter – it's like an ice skating rink. Ensure a build up of snow does not block vents and flues. This is a daily task and it is good practice to sweep the area around the motorhome as well to keep it clear, dry and ice free. There is nothing more frustrating than injuring yourself by falling over in the parking area.

A shovel is essential to dig your motorhome out of the snow, this sounds fun but a few days of freezing temperatures, high winds and blizzards will shorten the fuse of any camper.

Andy Glasgow clears snow from the roof. Photo: Sue Glasgow.

Winter fridge vents fitted. Photo: Andy Glasgow.

Storing Your Equipment

Whatever your chosen mountain pursuit it is likely to involve some wet, muddy clothes and some cumbersome or sharp equipment. Most people opt to dry clothes in the shower cubicle but you need to think about how you are going to hang them up. Boxes, lined with newspaper, are ideal for muddy boots. Skis have very sharp edges which

Store your equipment carefully. Photo: Andy Glasgow.

can easily mark fixtures and fittings, so you need to consider how you are going to store them. Some people attach their skis to their rear ladder, but if you leave any of your equipment outside you must make sure it is under lock and key.

Life On The Road

Once you are on the road it is important that you travel safely and carry out regular maintenance to stop issues becoming problems. Even summer travellers should consider that temperatures are lower up mountains.

Mountain resorts can be isolated with limited supplies. Out of season (spring and autumn) shops may be closed. In winter, Service Points may be frozen. Before arriving at your chosen resort, stop in the lower valleys to stock up with anything you may need. Fill up the water tank and extra water bottles if you carry them. Empty the toilet and the wastewater tank. Check the gas levels and fill up or exchange if necessary. Stock up with food but remember that some packet food will expand as you increase altitude so make sure it has enough space.

Driving Mountain Roads

Mountain roads are often narrow and twisty and it takes both skill and concentration to safely drive them. General etiquette dictates that on narrow mountain lanes the driver heading down hill is expected to pull over when traffic is met coming uphill. Driving with dipped headlights on during the day has significantly reduced accidents in those countries that it is obligatory. Sounding the horn on twisting roads with reduced visibility is highly recommended whilst mountain driving. Study maps and plan routes carefully as difficult

Mountain roads are often narrow and twisty.

or dangerous sections of roads are often marked and are best avoided. In winter and spring, high passes may be closed due to snow, snow drifts or wind. Never drive down a route marked as closed or open closed gates.

Driving down a mountain with a fully loaded motorhome takes a lot more skill than in a car, especially in snow. You have to descend slowly and utilise your gears, only using the brakes when necessary. Brake fade is the name given to loss of braking due to overheating. When brakes overheat this heat alters the characteristics of the compounds resulting in friction being lost and therefore reduced braking and induced fear. The warning signs are a strong chemical smell similar to burning electrics or metal being cut by an angle-grinder. Pulling over and allowing brakes to cool should make them function again but if they have reached the stage of smoke coming from the wheels it may be too late. If you have suffered brake fade and have any doubt on their condition get them checked by a qualified engineer.

Avoidance is always the best strategy so descend in the same gear you used to ascend, if third gear is too fast, instead of braking, change down to second gear. Do not rest your foot on the pedal but brake harder periodically.

Never drive a mountain route signed as closed.

When descending on snow and or ice remember that the brakes apply to all wheels whereas engine braking applies only to the driven wheels. Therefore, if you suddenly drop down a gear you may cause a loss of traction. Traction may also be lost if you apply harsh braking so be gentle. Don't worry about the local traffic. However fast you drive it will not be fast enough for them, so pull over where you can and let them past. Avoid departing from the ski resort exactly as the lifts close, or arriving just before the lifts open as you will be battling locals who won't appreciate you being there. Aim to drive during the day in clear weather. Always check the weather forecasts before departing and call in at local tourist offices to check the routes and resorts are open. Avoid, where possible, driving at night, in falling snow, high winds or fog.

Out And About

Winter visitors should have the latest edition of *Where to Ski and Snowboard* so they can assess the resorts. There are several walking guidebooks by Cicerone, Lonely Planet, and Sunflower Books which cover short and long walks. Tourist guides such as *French Alps* by Michelin provide information on tourist sites as well as some walks and drives.

Before engaging in any mountain pursuits make sure you do your homework. Ensure you have the correct insurance just in case mountain rescue is required. Ski insurance can be purchased with lift passes for €1/€2, however good travel insurance is always recommended. Check weather reports and pack clothes for all weather as it can change quickly in the mountains. Do not overestimate your ability and build in extra time as a contingency. Carry as much information as possible to navigate with, have maps and a compass and do not rely solely on pre-placed footpath markers. When possible let someone know where you are going and what time you will return.

Use maps and a compass and do not rely solely on pre-placed footpath markers.

CHAPTER 5 – Documentation

Knowing that everybody loves paperwork, we have made this chapter as vibrant as possible. Read this chapter carefully so that you understand the implications of what you are doing and what documentation you are legally required to travel with.

Passports And Identification

Your passport is the most important document that you travel with and may be the only documentation recognised as personal identification. Before you book your ferry, check that everybody travelling with you has an undamaged and valid passport that has an expiration date no less than six months after your intended return date. The following countries require you to carry your passport at all times as identification: Belgium, Bulgaria, Cyprus, Czech Republic, Estonia, The Netherlands, Slovakia, Bosnia and Herzegovina, Croatia, Montenegro and Serbia. When you are not required to carry your passport keep it in a secure place, preferably a safe, and avoid handing it over to anyone unless necessary. If you need to renew your British passport or have any passport related questions visit www.gov.uk/browse/abroad/passports.

The Camping Card International (CCI) is a credit card sized card that displays the holder's name, address, and passport number. The CCI is worth buying because it is common, across Europe, for campsite receptionists to ask for passports for identification when booking in and the CCI is an acceptable substitute for your passport. Sometimes receptionists wish to keep your documents overnight and it is preferable to let them keep your CCI rather than your passport. CCI cardholders also benefit from 2,500,000 Swiss Francs worth of third-party insurance against accidental damage at campsites. The CCI has a website that details country specific camping information, Offsite-Parking rules and a list of over 1,700 campsites offering discounted pitch fees to CCI holders. Not all Swedish campsites accept the CCI. Luckily, they have their own card called the Camping Card Scandinavia, available at all campsite receptions, which you must buy if you wish to stay at that campsite. CCI cards cost from £5.50 and are available from organisations affiliated to the AIT, FIA or FICC. The following UK organisations offer CCI to their members: The Caravan Club, www.caravanclub.co.uk, Tel: 01342 326944, The Motor Caravanners Club, http://motorcaravanners.eu, Tel: 01684 311677, The Camping & Caravanning Club, www.campingandcaravanningclub.co.uk,

Go Motorhoming and Campervanning

Tel: 0845 1307631, and the RAC, www.rac.co.uk, Tel: 08000 468375. The AA no longer sells the CCI, however AA personal members may purchase a CCI from The Caravan Club. Have the following information on hand when you phone: date of birth, place of birth, nationality, passport number, passport date of issue, and passport place of issue.

Pet Passports

The Pet Travel Scheme (PETS) allows you to take your dog, cat, or ferret to many European countries without quarantine. If you wish to travel with a different species of pet contact the Department for Environment, Food and Rural Affairs (DEFRA), see www.defra.gov.uk, Tel: 0207 2386951.

PETS requirements and limitations from the 1st January 2012:

Warning: enhanced interior security.

- Restricted to dogs, cats, and ferrets only.
- First, the animal must be microchipped, with an EU standard microchip.
- Next, complete a course of rabies vaccinations, (21-day movement restriction applies).
- Obtain an EU pet passport from an Official Veterinarian or from your local Animal Health and Veterinary Laboratories Office.
- Passports are designed to last the life of the animal. They confirm the microchip number, the date of implant, and the rabies vaccination record.
- Rabies vaccinations are valid for three years, to re-validate the passport a booster vaccination is needed before the expiration date of the previous vaccination.
- Only five pets per owner are allowed in transit at any one time (exceptions apply).

The PETS scheme allows you to travel with your pets without restriction to the following EU countries: Austria, Belgium, Bulgaria, Ceuta, Czech Republic, Denmark, Estonia, Finland, France, Germany, Gibraltar, Greece, Greenland, Hungary, Ireland (UK-based pets do not need a passport to enter Ireland and Irish pets do not need a passport to enter the UK), Italy, Latvia, Lithuania, Luxembourg, The Netherlands, Poland, Portugal, Romania, Slovakia, Slovenia, Spain, Sweden and the UK.

Under the Pet Travel Scheme, dogs entering the UK must be treated for tapeworm no less than 24 hours and not more than 120 hours (1-5 days) before they are scheduled to arrive. Dogs entering the UK directly from Finland, Ireland, Malta or Norway are exempt from treatment.

A qualified vet must carry out the treatment and record it in the pet passport. The record must include the practice stamp and vets' signature, the date and time administered, and the name of the product and manufacturer. Confirm that an approved/licensed veterinary medicine containing Praziquantel has been given in the treatment of Echinococcus multilocularis tapeworm. Visit www.defra.gov.uk/wildlife-pets/pets/travel/ for up-to-date information. www.passportforpets.co.uk provides details of suitable vets near ports, click on the red crosses on the map for vet names and phone numbers.

Pets must not have been taken outside of the PETS participating countries in the six calendar months before entering the UK. Failing to comply with the scheme will mean the animal will have to enter quarantine when it arrives in the UK. Quarantine separates you from your pet for six months and is expensive. Visit www.defra.gov.uk, Tel: 0207 2386951 for more detailed information before you travel as some countries require additional forms. Further information can also be found on the European Union website http://europa.eu/travel/pets.

UK resident dogs, cats and ferrets can enter Croatia, Gibraltar, Norway, San Marino and Switzerland with an EU pet passport. UK resident dogs, cats and ferrets can also travel to a range of non-EU European and worldwide countries and return to the UK without the need for quarantine, if your animal meets the conditions of the PETS scheme. Non-EU European countries include Andorra, Belarus, Bosnia-Herzegovina, Iceland, Liechtenstein, and the Russian Federation, whilst worldwide countries include Australia, New Zealand and the United States (mainland). You need to check the import regulations of that country which might be different from those of the PETS scheme and many countries require an Export Health Certificate and/or an import licence.

Cat in a flap. Photo: Andy Glasgow.

Not all ferries accept pets and special requirements and additional costs may apply. Enquire when you book your ferry and see www.defra.gov.uk for a range of ferry companies and ferry routes that allow pets to travel under the PETS scheme. Check your pet insurance covers your pet in Europe.

The white cliffs of Dover.

Escaping The UK

Leaving Britain involves crossing the sea and recently we have found it cheaper to purchase tickets direct with the ferry companies online rather than through brokers or clubs. Consider travelling on strange days to unusual places, as this can reduce ticket prices considerably. Avoid travelling on public holidays, UK or Europe, as ferry costs will be higher and you may struggle to find accommodation on your first night. The busiest and most expensive time to cross the channel is the August bank holiday weekend. Frequent travellers can block-book discounted return tickets with some operators. These tickets allow you to arrive at the chosen port without booking and the ferry company will allow you to travel on the next available crossing, although supplements apply at peak times.

Sometimes it is quicker, or cheaper, to use ferries instead of roads, so consider your options. Some overnight ferries can only be booked with a cabin. Some ferry operators allow you to camp-on-board, in your motorhome, so ask before you book a cabin. There are no ferries departing or arriving in the UK that allow camping-on-board.

Company	Ports and crossings	Contact details
Brittany Ferries	Portsmouth – France: Caen, Cherbourg, Le Havre, St Malo and Spain: Santander, Bilbao. Poole – Cherbourg (France). Plymouth – Roscoff, St Malo (France) and Santander (Spain). Cork – Roscoff (France).	www.brittany-ferries.co.uk Tel: 0871 2440744
DFDS	Dover – Dunkerque (France). Newcastle – Amsterdam (The Netherlands). Harwich – Esbjerg (Denmark). Portsmouth – Le Havre (France). Newhaven – Dieppe (France).	www.dfdsseaways.co.uk Tel: 0871 5747235
Euro Tunnel	Folkestone – Calais (France).	www.eurotunnel.com Tel: 0844 3353535
P&O Ferries	Dover – Calais (France). Hull – Rotterdam (The Netherlands) and Zeebrugge (Belgium). Liverpool – Dublin. Larne – Troon and Cairnryan.	www.poferries.com Tel: 08716 642121
MyFerryLink	Dover – Calais (France).	www.myferrylink.com Tel: 0844 2482100
Stena Line	Harwich – Hook Van Holland (The Netherlands). Ireland – Britain routes: Belfast – Cairnryan and Liverpool. Dublin and Dun Laoghaire – Holyhead. Rosslare – Fishguard.	www.stenaline.co.uk Tel: 08447 707070

A Brittany Ferries cabin.

Channel Tunnel, Folkestone.

Go Motorhoming and Campervanning

Ferry journeys cannot be compared to cruising and we have developed a ferry survival strategy for any crossing where we are obliged to leave the motorhome. On short crossings, we take a flask of tea. If the journey coincides with a mealtime, we either eat at an onboard restaurant or bring food with us. We always carry our laptop onboard so that we can watch a DVD and listen to it on headphones. We also pack the laptop charger and continental plug adaptor as it is often possible to sit near a plug socket. On longer journeys with a cabin we take the same kit but include more DVDs and take our electric kettle, teabags, UHT milk and five litres of drinking water.

Gas cylinders must be turned off during ferry journeys. On longer crossings it may be possible to plug the motorhome into an electric point so that the fridge can run. Sometimes the plug sockets are located in the deck roof and staff lower them with a pole, on other ferries they are on the walls. Sometimes electric cables crossing the deck are stuck down with adhesive tape for safety reasons.

Avoid the fjords area of Norway if you are not keen on ferries, as the roads frequently end abruptly and a ferry has to be taken to continue the journey. The ferry embarkation experience is normally confusing, but never more frantic than in Greece where you may be asked to reverse on or off a ferry. Beware of grounding when entering or exiting the ferry and be watchful for other motorists or pedestrians. Out of season, timetables at small ports should be treated more as guidance than fact. Tickets for long crossings can be purchased from brokers near the ports, or on board for short trips.

Travelling Within The European Union

European Union citizens and citizens from Norway, Iceland and Switzerland can travel and stay in another EU country for up to three months without a visa, providing they have a valid passport. This includes: Austria, Belgium, Bulgaria, Croatia, Cyprus, Czech Republic, Denmark, Estonia, Finland, France, Germany, Greece, Hungary, Ireland, Italy, Latvia, Lithuania, Luxembourg, Malta, The Netherlands, Poland, Portugal, Romania, Slovakia, Slovenia, Spain, Sweden, UK, Norway, Iceland and Switzerland. EU citizens have the right to reside in another EU country, however, if they intend to stay for three months or more they are obliged to register residency with that country, although failing to register does not remove the right to reside in the country. This legislation is of little consequence to EU citizens travelling around Europe unless they intend to reside permanently in another country.

Some borders in Europe are little more than a sign due to the Schengen Agreement.

Since 1995, travellers have been enjoying an increasingly borderless Europe thanks to the Schengen Agreement. There are border controls when entering and exiting the Schengen area, but once entered people are allowed to travel between member countries without the inconvenience of border checks. Currently, 25 countries form the Schengen zone: Austria, Belgium, Czech Republic, Denmark, Estonia, Finland, France, Germany, Greece, Hungary, Iceland, Italy, Latvia, Lithuania, Luxembourg, Malta, The Netherlands, Norway, Poland, Portugal, Slovakia, Slovenia, Spain, Sweden, and Switzerland.

The Schengen system was absorbed into EU law in 1999 within the Amsterdam Treaty. Despite this, the United Kingdom and Ireland are exempt from adopting the Schengen system. Although the Schengen area does not have internal borders, officials have the right to ask you to identify yourself by showing your passport or ID card. Be aware that driving licences, post, bank, or tax cards may not be accepted as identification. Countries can reinstate borders should they wish to, but this is unusual.

Australian, Canadian, New Zealand, and USA passport holders without criminal records do not need to apply for a Schengen visa for visits of less than 90 days. Although a physical visa is not required, passport checks will be recording your movements in and out of the Schengen area. This has the same effect as if you had category C Schengen visa and a category C Schengen visa limits non-EU citizens to a maximum of 90 days over a 180-day period, from the date of entry into the Schengen area. You can come and go as you please during the 180-day period as long as you do not exceed 90 days within the Schengen area. Once the first 180-day period has elapsed, you can start again. Exceeding three months is treated as illegal residency and being caught could result in a fine, deportation, possibly a criminal record and registration as an offender on the Schengen Information System (SIS).

Observant readers will have noted above that the UK and Ireland are not part of the Schengen area despite being in the EU. Australian, New Zealand, United States and Canadian tourists can visit the UK for up to six months visa free and be out of the Schengen area. You can also visit Albania, Belarus, Bosnia and Herzegovina, Former Yugoslav Republic of Macedonia, Moldova, Montenegro, Russia, Serbia and the Ukraine or maybe include a trip to Morocco. Remember to obtain the necessary visas to visit these countries and to get your passport stamped every time you enter or exit the Schengen area to ensure you can prove you have not outstayed your welcome.

Visa requirements are complicated and subject to changes and conditions. Always check you have current information by contacting the relevant embassies before you travel. Further information on the Schengen agreement and travelling within the European Union can be found at http://ec.europa.eu/dgs/home-affairs/what-we-do/policies/borders-and-visas.

Travelling Outside The European Union

British passport holders travelling outside the EU will need to check entry requirements and read the advice given at the foreign office website www.gov.uk/foreign-travel-advice. Ensure you get your passport stamped on entry and exit.

At the time of publication, 90-day tourist visas were automatically given to British passport holders upon entry into the following countries: Albania, Andorra, Bosnia and Herzegovina, Georgia, Iceland, Kosovo (although visitors may need to prove why they are visiting), Liechtenstein, Macedonia, Moldova, Montenegro, Morocco, Norway, Serbia, Switzerland, Tunisia and Ukraine.

Armenia, Azerbaijan, the Russian Federation, and Turkey all require British passport holders to obtain visas. Visas may need to be applied for in advance so confirm this before you leave home. Ensure that your passport is valid for six months after your entry and that you obtain a stamp in your passport at the point of entry and exit.

British passport holders require a visa to visit Australia. Applications can be made online for free at www.immi.gov.au/visitors/tourist/evisitor and be notification of the visa result is sent to you via email. If you are over 75 you may need to undergo a health check for your tourist visa, visit www.immi.gov.au/allforms/health-requirements. British passport holders visiting New Zealand for less than six months do not need a visa providing an onward ticket has been booked and the passport is valid for at least one month after the visit.

British passport holders can visit the United States for 90 days without a visa through the Visa Waiver Programme (VWP). Visitors must register with the VWP website in advance of their trip at https://esta.cbp.dhs.gov and pay an administration charge of around $14.00. They will then be notified if they can visit the United States without a visa. British passport holders can visit Canada without a visa but ensure you have at least six months validity on your passport after your intended return.

Non-British passport holders need to check their entry requirements before visiting the above countries. Visa information is usually provided by your government. Australian passport holders should visit www.dfat.gov.au, New Zealand passport holders should visit www.safetravel.govt.nz, United States passport holders should visit http://travel.state.gov/travel, and Canadian passport holders should visit www.voyage.gc.ca.

Driving Licences

Anyone intending to drive abroad must have their full valid driving licence with them. Provisional, expired or disqualified driving licences do not entitle the holder to drive abroad. Driving licences issued in the EU allow an EU citizen to drive anywhere in the EU in any vehicle the holder is entitled to drive.

Photo-card licences are issued in most countries and people with the old paper British driving licence may need to show their passport as photo identification. It is recommended that paper licences be surrendered to the DVLA for replacement with a photo licence; alternatively buy an International Driving Permit. If you have a British photo driving licence, you must travel with both the plastic card and supporting paper copy. Photo licences are valid for 10 years from the date of issue, the date of renewal is marked on the licence so check now.

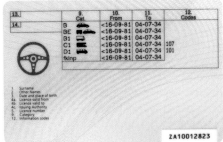

UK driving licence front. Image DVLA.   UK driving licence rear. Image DVLA.

Driving licences detail the category of vehicles the holder is entitled to drive, any restrictions and penalties. Your licence may be requested at a roadside check, if stopped for a traffic violation, involved in an accident, or by vehicle hire staff. If you passed your driving test in Britain before the 1 January 1997, unless restrictions apply, your licence will be for category B and C1E. This allows you to drive a vehicle with a MAM weight of 7,500kg and a GTW weight up to 8,250kg if towing a trailer. Drivers reaching the age of 70 will lose any entitlement to drive vehicles over 3500kg, unless a medical is taken, passed, and submitted to the DVLA.

If you have passed your driving test since 1 January 1997, you have a category B licence and are entitled to drive a vehicle with a MAM of 3,500kg plus a 750kg trailer. Braked trailers over 750kg may be towed if the combined weight of the vehicle and trailer does not exceed 3,500kg, but the trailer MAM must be lighter than the tow vehicle unladen weight. If you wish to drive a vehicle heavier than 3500kg you need to take a C1 driving test. Further information regarding driving licences and online forms are available from www.gov.uk/browse/driving or pick up a form from a Post Office.

International Driving Permits (IDP) are not needed in the EU if you have a British photo driving licence. A current list of countries that require an International Driving Permit is available on the application form or suppliers' websites. At the time of publishing, the list contained the following European countries: Albania, Belarus, Bosnia, Bulgaria, Croatia, Czech Republic, Georgia, Iceland, Kazakhstan, Macedonia, Montenegro, Romania, The Russian Federation, Serbia, Slovenia, Turkey and Ukraine. British driving licence holders are advised to carry an International Driving Permit if driving in Australia, Canada, Morocco, Tunisia and the United States.

The International Driving Permit displays a photo of the driver and the text is printed in several languages. They can only be issued to valid driving licence holders over the age of 18 and are valid for 12 months. You can purchase one from the AA (www.theaa.com) or the RAC (www.rac.co.uk) and the Post Office (www.postoffice.co.uk). Non-EU driving licence holders are recommended to obtain an IDP from their automotive association before they travel to Europe. Even if you travel with an International Driving Permit you will still need to take your current driving licence with you.

Vehicle Requirements

Automotive and traffic law is not completely harmonised across the EU, but a vehicle compliant with the laws of the registered country is usually accepted in another EU country for up to six months. This means your UK registered road vehicles must have valid road tax, insurance and MOT. If you intend to keep a vehicle in a single EU country longer than six months visit http://ec.europa.eu/youreurope/citizens/vehicles/registration/ for further information.

MOT

UK legislation requires privately used motorhomes over three years old to pass an annual class IV (4) environmental and road safety inspection, known in the UK as an MOT. An MOT must be carried out at a registered

MOT testing bay at Eric Road Test Centre, Dover.

Department of Transport testing station. The initial three year period when an MOT is not required is calculated from the date of first registration with the DVLA. Vehicles can be MOT'd at any time whether or not the current MOT has expired. A vehicle can be MOT'd up to 31 days in advance so the new one starts as the existing expires, therefore 13 months MOT is possible. If you intend to carry goods for commercial activity, your motorhome needs to pass a class VII (7) MOT if the motorhome weighs between 3000kg and 3500kg, or tested as a goods vehicle if it weighs over 3500kg. There has been some confusion amongst the motorhome community whether or not such things as scooters used for pleasure are deemed as goods. The Vehicle and Operator Services Agency (VOSA) who oversee MOT testing, provided us with the following statement: *'In our view anything that the driver and his friends or family might reasonably be taking to use recreationally on their trip would be fine. Anything that they are taking either to sell or to use in any commercial activity may not be, depending on the particular circumstances... As far as we are aware there have been no cases of the Police treating [recreational] items as goods when carried on a motorhome.'*

There are no approved MOT testing stations outside of the UK and equivalent foreign tests, including tests in British overseas territories such as Gibraltar, are not accepted. If you are planning to be away when your vehicle either requires its first or annual MOT inspection, you have no choice but to bring it back to the UK. Eric Road Test Centre in Dover has an MOT bay that is suitable for motorhomes up to 5000kg and no taller than 3.63m (11'11"). Both class IV and VII tests can be taken. You can book an MOT test online at www.motdover.co.uk or by phone on (0044) 01304 242233. Eric Road Test Centre, Eric Road, Dover, CT17 0TE, N51°08.133' E001°17.835'.

Road Fund Licence

Every UK road-registered vehicle must display a valid tax disc when on the public highway, whether being driven in the UK or Europe. Renewal tax discs, valid for either six or twelve months, can be purchased two months in advance. To obtain a tax disc the vehicle must have a current MOT and be insured. Whilst abroad it is easy to renew your tax disc online as the DVLA website instantly checks that the vehicle has valid MOT and insurance. The tax disk is posted, within five working days, to the registered keepers address only, but can be forwarded to you or collected if you have to return to the UK for an MOT. If your motorhome MOT and tax disc do not expire in the same month, you can surrender the tax disc to the DVLA during the month you have your motorhome MOT'd. The DVLA will refund the value of each whole month and you can purchase a new tax disc, thus adjusting any imbalance between MOT and road tax. Concessionary rates apply and all vehicle tax information is available at the Post Office or on www.gov.uk/browse/driving/car-tax-discs.

Having a valid UK road tax disc does not exempt you from paying road tolls in Europe. Mostly tolls are chargeable on motorways and on some bridges. The AA website (www.theaa.com) provides toll road information. Countries such as Austria that have a one-off charge are detailed in the country guides at www.go-motorhoming.co.uk. Be aware there is a time limit on some toll roads and this should be shown on the ticket. In Portugal you must exit the toll road within 12 hours and within 24 hours on French autoroutes. Failing to do so may result in additional charges. We strongly advise against spending the night at a motorway service station because of the risk of burglary and the possibility of exceeding time restrictions.

Chris paying a French toll by credit card.

Low emission zones, congestion charges, and exclusion zones are now common in large European cities. Each country has its own rules and regulations, thus specific country and city research is necessary. www.lowemissionzones.eu details the low emission zones within the EU and further details are provided on www.go-motorhoming.co.uk.

Check your toll ticket, this one for the A1 in Portugal clearly indicates that you must complete your journey within 12 hours.

Insurance

There are plenty of insurance companies and policies to choose from, and even more variations in the level of cover provided. Your first choice is whether or not you want comprehensive insurance that covers the cost of repairs if the motorhome is accidently damaged, or provides compensation should your motorhome be written-off or stolen. Most people buy insurance that provides comprehensive cover in the UK and Europe, but check that the Europe cover is not reduced to Third Party, Fire and Theft. Some policies restrict European travel to as little as 30 days, although most now offer 180 days. Some policies that state they offer 365 days European cover do not allow this to be taken continuously. Some insurance policies are designed for cars, so check whether specialist items such as awnings are insured and that the value of contents insurance is sufficient; realistically this needs to be at least £3,000. Some insurance policies have age restrictions for drivers under 30 or over 75 years old or do not insure vehicles over 25 years old. Always check the small print and make sure the following are provided:

- The motorhome will be repatriated (brought home) if you become incapable of driving it, or it is not roadworthy following an accident.
- A 24-hour, 365-days-a-year English language helpline is available.
- That an alternative motorhome or accommodation is offered in the event of an accident or loss.
- A bail bond is offered should the vehicle be impounded after an accident in Spain.

Confirm the following:

- Territorial limits. What countries are covered and what level of cover? Usually all EU countries will be offered at the same level of cover. Check whether European cover is comprehensive and check how you get green cards for additional countries.
- What factors invalidate your insurance? Travelling without a current tax disc, MOT or exceeding the vehicle weight limits will probably invalidate your insurance.
- Check whether annual mileage is restricted.
- If vehicle recovery is included what happens if the motorhome breaks down? Are roadside repairs undertaken or are you simply recovered to the nearest garage?

Some insurance brokers offer motorhome-specific policies. Comfort Insurance offers a policy with 365 days continuous travel. This policy is suitable for people living in their motorhome Full-Time in the UK and Europe and who may have no fixed address, visit www.comfort-insurance.co.uk, Tel: 0800 0304206. The Camping and Caravanning Club can offer 365 days continuous EU cover as long as it is requested and is restricted to motorhomers up to the age of 80, Tel: 08451 307631 visit www.campingandcaravanningclub.co.uk. Saga specialises in insurance for the over 50s and has no upper age limit, visit www.saga.co.uk, Tel: 0800 0964553. Adrian Flux specialises in providing insurance for the unusual and old such as classic VW campervans, self-build and unusual conversions, RVs and high-end European motorhomes, visit www.adrianflux.co.uk, Tel: 0800 3698590. DownUnder Insurance Services provides insurance for British registered vehicles owned by Australians, Americans, Canadians, New Zealanders and South Africans over 20 years old and Brits over 25. Policies allow up to 12 months' travel in the UK and Europe in vehicles younger than 32 years, free from major modifications and with no more than seven seats. Up to four named drivers can be registered on the policy, visit www.duinsure.com, Tel: 0800 393908. Day Insure provide short-term cover, 28 days or less for UK-registered vehicles, visit www.dayinsure.com.

The following insurance providers also offer motorhome specific insurance policies: The Caravan Club, www.caravanclub.co.uk, Tel: 01342 326944, The Motorcaravanners Club, http://motorcaravanners.eu, Tel: 01684 311677, Safeguard, www.safeguarduk.co.uk, Tel:0800 9775954, Caravan Guard www.caravanguard.co.uk, Tel: 0800 1488400, Towergate, www.towergateinsurance.co.uk, Tel: 0844 8921413, and Campton, www.campton.co.uk, Tel:01883 742460.

Insurance policies issued within the EU must provide the minimum insurance cover required by law in every EU country. Third-party insurance is the minimum level of insurance required in any EU country, but your motorhome will actually be covered comprehensively if you have that type of policy. Your motorhome Certificate of Motor Insurance lists the countries covered within the territorial limits. Should you wish to travel to a country not in the territorial limits you will need to purchase an International Motor Insurance Card, know as a Green Card. A Green Card proves that you have the minimum legal requirements for third party liability insurance required by law in a specific country. The Green Card system operates in Europe and countries bordering the Mediterranean and Green Cards are required in Albania, Belarus, Bosnia and Herzegovina, Former Yugoslav Republic of

Macedonia, Montenegro, Morocco, Russia, Serbia, Tunisia, Turkey and Ukraine. Green Cards can often be purchased from your insurance provider in advance or local insurance can be purchased at the border of the country. It is worth noting that your insurance provider may not provide you with an actual green card when they send you your insurance documents, some simply print an explanation on the reverse of your Certificate of Motor Insurance in multiple languages stating that Green Card cover is provided. However an actual Green Card is still a widely recognised document throughout Europe and is most likely to be recognised and understood should you have an accident. If you wish to have a physical Green Card, your insurance company should be able to send you one upon request. The Motor Insurers' Bureau (www.mib.org.uk) administers the Green Card system in the UK but does not provide Green Card insurance.

Police or ministry check points occur all over Europe and a vigilant motorist will notice that oncoming vehicles usually flash to indicate the presence of a speed trap or check point. Vehicles that are pulled over will be inspected and the officials will be looking for the essential items listed at the beginning of Chapter 4 as well as any vehicle defects. Some countries have additional regulations, for example in winter Germany requires all vehicles to be fitted with winter or all season tyres and some countries ban speed camera detectors or satellite navigators with activated speed camera locations. The AA website provides details of vehicle requirements, drink drive limits, radar detector laws, seatbelt laws and fines at www.theaa.com/motoring_advice/overseas/index.html.

Signs may indicate speed cameras. Many countries prohibit the use of speed camera detection equipment and the speed camera function should be disabled on your satellite navigator.

Police issuing charges for vehicle or driving offences will normally collect fines on-the-spot.

A new database called EU CAR Information service (EUCARIS) enables vehicle and driving licence data to be exchanged within the EU. The level data provided varies country to country but is in increasing, see www.eucaris.net/participation for up-to-date information. In April 2013, France, Belgium, The Netherlands, Germany and Switzerland only, were exchanging vehicle and owner data for the enforcement of traffic violation and unpaid tolls. Outstanding fines do not go away so if you return to a country and are stopped by the police it is likely that unpaid fines and additional late payment penalties may be applied. EU countries may request through the courts the contact details of an offender that has fine over €70.

Vehicle Recovery

Broken-down motorhomes may not be able to be recovered by standard recovery trucks due to the motorhomes weight and the rear overhang. The overhang normally prevents towing on a hydraulic lift system, where the front wheels are lifted off the ground, as the rear of the motorhome could get damaged. Instead a vehicle designed for recovering commercial vehicles may have to be used. Rigid or rope towing systems may be suitable for a short distance as long as the towing vehicle is sufficiently large. Automatic vehicles cannot be towed unless the drive wheels are of the road. Some recovery companies will not recover vehicles they deem be overweight. Whenever you contact your recovery company for assistance advise them of your vehicle's weight and dimensions.

Standard recovery trucks, like this one, may not be able to recover large motorhomes thankfully campervans are no problem.

On Christmas day, whilst driving in Normandy, France, our brakes completely failed but we were able to stop safely. After phoning and making arrangements with our recovery company we were transported, along with the motorhome, to a garage and abandoned outside for the night. The next day the garage opened, inspected the brakes and ordered the parts. On the third day the €500 repairs were completed. The recovery company organised everything professionally and made sure that we were taken to a garage where someone spoke some English. We do feel that €500 was a lot for a replacement brake calliper and new rear brake shoes, but what choice did we have?

Breakdown recovery may be offered with motorhome insurance or it can be bought independently. Wherever you buy breakdown recovery, clearly state the dimensions and weight of your motorhome ensuring that they can and will recover it, you may wish to have this confirmed in writing. Confirm the territorial limits, as some companies exclude some Green Card countries. Ensure you understand the level of UK and European breakdown assistance provided. Roadside assistance may not be available in Europe and the motorhome may be taken to the nearest garage regardless of the fault. Confirm how many continuous days continental travel are covered. Some policies offer a trip total and annual total. The following chart provides a snapshot of some restrictions applied by recovery companies.

Organisation	Duration restrictions	Weight restrictions	Width restrictions	Length restrictions	Height restrictions	Territorial limitations
Caravan Club Mayday	None	None	None	None	None	UK
Caravan Club Red Pennant	32 days per trip	3,850kg	2.3m – 7'6"	7.32m – 24'0"	3m – 9'10"	EU +
AA UK	None	3,500kg	2.3m – 7'6"	None	None	UK
AA Europe	365 days	3,500kg	2.3m – 7'6"	7m – 23'0"	3m – 9'10"	EU +
RAC UK	None	3,500kg	2.3m – 7'6"	5.5m – 18'0"	None	UK
RAC Europe	90 days	3,500kg	2.25m – 7'4"	7m – 23'0"	3m – 9'10"	EU +
Camping and Caravanning Club, Arrival (RAC)	90 days	None	None	None	None	EU +
Green Flag	90 days	3,500kg	2.55m 8'4"	7m – 23'0"	3m - 9'10"	EU +

The Caravan Club's Red Pennant Overseas Motoring Cover can be adjusted to suit individual member requirements at a cost. They cover motorhomes up to 15 years old, www.caravanclub.co.uk, Tel: 01342 326944. The AA charges an older vehicle supplement for all vehicles over six years old, www.theaa.com, Tel: 0800 0852721. The RAC offers cover for vehicles up to 11 years old at the start of the journey, www.rac.co.uk, Tel: 0800 0156000. Green Flag cover vehicles less than 16 years old, www.greenflag.com, Tel: 0845 2462766.

Personal Health And Wellbeing

The European Health Insurance Card (EHIC) allows UK citizens to access medical care at state hospitals within the EEC. You may have to pay for treatment at reduced cost and then seek reimbursement in the UK. The EHIC replaces and invalidates all previous E111 forms. The EHIC can be applied for online at www.ehic.org.uk or a form can be acquired from the Post Office. The EHIC card is valid for five years and can be renewed up to six months before the expiry date. The EHIC does not cover the cost of returning you to the UK, mountain rescue, or any treatment carried out by private healthcare organisations.

Personal medical insurance is not a legal requirement, but it is advisable to have when travelling, especially if you are not an EU citizen or if you intend to travel outside of the EU. Independent motorhomers should remember there is no tour rep or travel company support.

Ensure your personal insurance provides at least the following:
• Fly you home if medically required.
• Fly out relatives if you are ill or imprisoned.
• Repatriate your body.
• Provide search and rescue.
• Provide adequate medical cover.
• Fly you home for a relative's funeral (although you are unlikely to be more than three days drive from the UK).
• Provide cover for sports and activities such as bicycling, walking, swimming, or travelling in someone else's car. Could you go horse riding, skiing, windsurfing, or canoeing? Dangerous sports are covered if required, but be aware of what is not covered.

Go Motorhoming and Campervanning

People with existing medical conditions can obtain insurance from All Clear to Travel, visit www.allcleartravel.co.uk, Tel: 0845 2505350. Saga covers pre-existing medical conditions and state no upper age limit, visit www.saga.co.uk, Tel: 0800 0158055. Free Spirit Travel Insurance provide travel insurance for people over 80 years old, visit www.free-spirit.com, Tel: 0845 230 5000. www.travelhealth.co.uk details other insurers.

Many high street companies provide travel insurance, but we recommend you look at comprehensive travel insurance policies available to independent travellers. STA Travel provides travel insurance for people 65 or younger, www.statravel.co.uk, Tel: 0333 3210099. Endsleigh will insure people under 65 years old for 365 day's travel and 65-74 year olds for 183 days per year, visit www.endsleigh.co.uk, Tel: 0800 0283571. Saga offers travel insurance to people over 50 and has no upper age limit, visit www.saga.co.uk, Tel: 0800 0158055. Be aware that these policies may be voided if you return to the United Kingdom for more than 24 hours. So if you are planning to return, only book insurance to that point, it can always be extended if your plans change. Check the small print to see if your insurance is invalidated by any activities, such as consuming alcohol. Generally travel cover is not provided in countries designated a 'war zone' or 'unsafe', so check the Foreign Office website regularly (www.gov.uk/fco) for details of countries that British citizens are advised not to travel to.

We recommend that you have vaccinations against infections spread via faecal matter. Cross-contamination could occur at combined toilet emptying and water collection points, both at campsites and at Motorhome Stopovers. We have witnessed, all too often, the spout of a toilet cassette being placed over the fresh water tap during rinsing. The following diseases can be spread via faecal matter and can be vaccinated against: Hepatitis A, Cholera,

This Service Point has one tap so cross-contamination is likely.

Fill your fresh water tank from taps marked 'Drinking Water'.

Polio, and you should confirm that your tetanus and diphtheria vaccinations are up-to-date. These injections are usually free on the NHS and some are simply boosters required every 10 years as part of the NHS vaccination programme if you were vaccinated as a child.

Other diseases found in Europe that you might consider vaccinating against include Rabies, spread by animal bites and Tick Borne Encephalitis, spread by tick bites and unpasteurised milk. Some vaccinations require a course of injections over a month or more and may have to be specially ordered. Any vaccination not available on the NHS can be bought from your doctor or a travel clinic, such as MASTA, visit www.masta-travel-health.com.

Europe has resident mosquitoes and, although these are unlikely to carry malaria, before you depart seek medical advice based on the countries you intend to visit, www.gov.uk/fco. Mosquito bites can be itchy and uncomfortable and they often develop into aggravated penny sized reactions. Pack insect repellent, after bite, and antihistamines in your medical kit. Scandinavia, especially Finland, appears to have the most ferocious mosquitoes, but more Brits are bitten in Spain. A mosquito head cover is worth buying if visiting northern Scandinavia in summer. Individual country information and vaccination advice can be found at www.fitfortravel.nhs.uk and www.travelhealth.co.uk.

BEAT THE **BITE**
'Mosquitoes can cause Disease'

When outdoors at dusk and dawn:
Cover up with loose clothing
and use repellent
An initiative of the regional Public Health Unit and local Shire Councils

Australian mozzie warning.

Travel with sufficient prescription and over-the-counter medicines for your trip. Carry your prescription to provide evidence to authorities if required. You may be able to buy drugs from

Pharmacies are usually indicated by an illuminated green cross.

pharmacies for self-medication if you know the active ingredient name. European pharmacists often sell what would be prescription medicines in the UK and will assist as much as language allows.

European pharmacists are clearly signed by a green cross, or a blue Star of Life. Drugs are expensive in Germany and Italy and inexpensive in Greece, Spain, and Andorra. Medical advice is provided on www.nhsdirect.nhs.uk. Campsite receptions and tourist information offices should provide contact details of local doctors. Explaining problems can be difficult and you may have to wait for an English-speaking doctor. People with pre-existing medical conditions may wish to identify this with jewellery displaying a Star of Life. UTAG produce USB drives designed to be worn around your neck or on your wrist, and a card version to carry in your wallet. The Star of Life symbol is clearly displayed and the USB drive can be loaded with your medical data and any other digital data, visit www.utagice.com for more details.

Finance, Budgeting And Keeping Costs Down

£250 is the minimum weekly budget required for two people actively touring with a motorhome. Restrained spending is required as this includes food, fuel, accommodation, repairs, tourism, literally everything except insurance. When touring Scandinavia, expect to spend £300 per week as the cost of living and unavoidable ferry crossings stretch the budget. To stay within these figures you will not be able to eat out often, go to every tourist site, or stay in campsites every night. If you stay on one campsite for an extended period you can expect to spend £150-£200 per week, around £750 per month. If your budget is tight, log your expenses daily in a cashbook, some people will find this interesting irrespective of budget. Working whilst travelling may be part of your plan, but it will take quite a lot of effort to find suitable work. Jobs generally fall into two categories, lifestyle jobs or short-term cash jobs. Neither is well paid but lifestyle jobs allow the continuation of a lifestyle choice. Some campsite wardens work during the summer and tour the rest of the year, or spend the winter in Spain. Campsite wardens work when everyone else is on holiday; they clean toilets, mow grass, do office work, and need good customer service skills. Detailed information about becoming a warden for The Caravan Club is available at www.caravanclub.co.uk. The Camping and Caravanning Club also has warden positions, www.campingandcaravanningclub.co.uk/about-us/jobs whilst privately owned campsites advertise jobs on www.ukcampsite.co.uk/jobs and www.caravan-jobfinder.co.uk.

House sitting may provide you with some income. HG Security employs motorhome owners to guard empty property. Training and certification is required for this job, visit www.hgsecurity.co.uk. Another website, www.mindmyhouse.com, matches house sitters with house owners. Most sitters offer their services for free and house owners are expected to cover reasonable utility costs. Jobs in the travel industry are generally very competitive and you will have to work very hard to become a paid writer in magazines. There are limited opportunities for guidebook inspectors and tour leaders for motorhome holidays, and it is advisable to contact the company you wish to work for directly to register your interest and availability.

People that like to be outside and do not mind hard work may consider fruit picking. Many farms in the UK need fruit pickers from June to October. Pickers are required in France to harvest grapes in the autumn and payment is around €50 per day including board and lodging, information can be found at www.pickingjobs.com. Organic farms worldwide take on voluntary workers in exchange for board and lodging, visit www.wwoof.org, www.seasonworkers.com advertises seasonal jobs such as ski instructor, chalet maid, or campsite cleaner. Entrepreneurial campers have run small businesses from their motorhomes for example hairdressing, soft toy making, retailing electrical goods, and artists who paint scenes on motorhomes. Check with reception before you start working from your pitch. EU citizens can work freely in the EU, but visitors from outside the EU should check their visas.

Euros are the principal currency in Europe, even outside the euro zone, having replaced American dollars. If you intend to take travellers' cheques ensure they are in euros, saving on double transactions. It is advisable to take a small amount of euros in cash when you depart the United Kingdom and keep a small amount of sterling for your return. Visa and MasterCard

Visa and MasterCard are usually accepted, but American Express is rarely accepted in Europe. Who knows if this Road House in Western Australia accepts the cards that 'are NOT EXCEPTED'.

credit and debit cards are widely accepted in most countries except The Netherlands and Germany. American Express is rarely accepted. There is no need to obtain large amounts of euros before you travel as ATMs, commonly known as cash machines, are widely available across Europe at service stations, banks and supermarkets. Most towns should have at least one ATM, but they are rare in villages or rural communities. Most ATMs offer a choice of languages, so the transaction can take place in English. Bank ATM's rarely charge for transactions, however ATMs found in shops and garages often do, a message is normally displayed detailing charges, so it's your choice. Withdrawing cash on your credit card will incur charges. Check that your bank cards will remain valid for the duration of your trip. Do not forget to pay your credit card's monthly bill by direct debit, or pay a lump sum into your credit card account before departure.

Spend a few hours checking the foreign currency bank charges and exchange rates offered by the high street banks. Frequent or long-term travellers could save considerable amounts of money by opening and using a favourable account, see www.metrobankonline.co.uk. Check for the following charges:

- Withdrawing money from a continental ATM machine, ideally this should be free.
- Making a purchase using your debit/credit card, ideally this should be free.
- The exchange rate offered by the card, this will be a figure that changes

daily (sometimes hourly), ideally you want a rate better than the tourist rate. To check the figure offered by the bank you will need to check that figure against other currency providers such as the Post Office or a travel agent on the same day.

• Ask if there are any additional charges, such as a commission charge for changing the money from sterling (£) to euros.

Pre-paid euro debit cards operate on a pay-as-you-go basis. When you top up, sterling is converted to euros and is spent using the debit card when abroad. This means that you can top up when exchange rates are favourable or use it as a saving method to help pay for your trip. This type of card may offer better exchange rates and charges than your current debit/credit card. Check if the pre-loaded card has an application fee or a top-up fee. Several companies offer pre-paid euro cards including www.caxtonfxcard.com, Tel:0845 222 2639 and www.travelex.co.uk, Tel: 0845 8727627.

When entering non-euro currency countries cash can usually be withdrawn from an ATM at the first town or fuel station. Do not panic, as euros are often accepted near borders although not necessarily at a good exchange rate. Careful cash withdrawal management will avoid the use of bureau de change and double transactions, for example changing sterling into euros into lev. Placing sole responsibility of money outside the euro zone to one person should avoid departing the country with money left over.

Meli finds time for trip planning during lunch.

Supermarkets usually have the cheapest fuel.

Well-known tourist sites are often expensive and lesser-known sites are often free. Repeated occupations, strategic marriages, and millennia of cross-border trade have enabled copycat architecture across Europe. The Greek temples in Sicily rival those found in Greece, and there appears to be an 'English Garden' in every European country. Most people decide upon their destination first, but we believe that you should focus on what you are going to see and do day-to-day and let that guide you. Buy your tourist information guidebooks and do your research in advance. Choose the sites you wish to visit, and then plan your route, as this will prevent unnecessary miles criss-crossing a country or continent. Free sites are detailed in country and, to a greater extent, regional guidebooks whereas Europe-wide guidebooks will focus on the major tourist-trap attractions.

Generally, fuel is most expensive on the motorways and cheapest at supermarket fuel stations, with a difference between 10-15 cents. Access into supermarket fuel stations is often restricted due to height barriers, low canopies, or limited space, so proceed with caution. When approaching borders look at the number plates of cars in the fuel stations and supermarkets, this indicates which country has cheaper fuel or food. In southern Italy you have to be particularly vigilant as often the price advertised is only for the pump marked Fia Dante, the others are up to 10 cents per litre more. Fuel also tends to be cheaper in principalities, such as Andorra and the Grand Duchy of Luxemburg. Diesel is predominantly cheaper than petrol in Europe. The Drive Alive website details current fuel prices across Europe, www.drive-alive.co.uk/fuel_prices_europe.html, and www.prix-carburants.gouv.fr shows fuel prices across France.

Unfortunately, the size of your motorhome will affect your budget. Motorhomes over 6m long or over 3,500kg can be considered large and heavy and additional charges often apply for pitches, tolls and ferries. Motorhomes with twin axles and or trailers also attract additional charges.

In several European countries motorhomes over 3,500kg pay higher tolls, Austria being a prime example, failing to pay the correct fee can result in a large fine. To keep travel costs down, avoid toll roads and use the local roads instead. When money is tight, you can forget going to Norway because there is often no option but to pay tolls and catch ferries.

Large campsites normally have onsite shops, where, as you might expect you pay for convenience. Some small campsites may sell only local wine or fresh bread, which you may have to order the night before. When you are staying at Motorhome Stopovers you should shop locally as much as possible, but when you are paying to stop at campsites this moral obligation is negated. There are hypermarkets across Europe and most don't have height restrictions, so it is possible to stock up before going to campsites. Continental signing laws allow hypermarkets to provide directional signs from great distances, so they are easy to find. As in the United Kingdom, supermarket prices vary and some offer discounts on fuel when you shop in store. Buying long-life products such as UHT milk reduces the need to shop regularly. Make the most of your fridge by removing bulky packaging. Prevent messy spills by keeping items in the fridge in sealed containers; plastic take away containers are ideal. Ensure milk and other liquids have pop down or screw tops, rather than a tear off opening although a peg can be used to seal the opening. In many continental supermarkets, especially Scandinavia, they either do not have, or charge for, carrier bags. Fold up cloth bags are stronger than carrier bags, and more practical when walking or cycling with shopping.

Communication

English and German are the two main tourist languages spoken across Europe. Most campsite receptions and tourist offices will have an English speaker. The Dutch and the Swiss are very useful for translation as they generally speak both English and German. The Italians will speak to you whether or not they speak English or you speak Italian. Out of respect, you should learn how to say hello in the country's language then ask if anyone speaks English. You may also wish to learn how to say that you have not learnt any more of their language. Start a conversation this way, no matter how bad your pronunciation or limited your vocabulary and people respond well, especially if they are hesitant to speak English. If you intend to travel predominantly in one country then learning that language would be useful. If you cannot attend a language course, then language CDs will give you basic knowledge and provide entertainment whilst driving. In any country it is worth learning the basics of 'hello', 'goodbye', 'please', 'thank you', and 'I would like'. Many guidebooks provide these basic words, nevertheless buying a language dictionary is money well spent.

The most reliable way to receive post whilst abroad is to have it sent to a campsite or domestic address. Vicarious Books sends books by airmail all over Europe and the success rate is better than 99 per cent. The unreliable element is the delivery time as some books are received within two days and some take one month. There is no pattern to the delivery times so make sure you plan for delays. Spain has the most unreliable post and often 'returns to sender' any mail with an incorrect address or postcode. Post can be sent 'Poste Restante' to a post office of your choice, but Vicarious Books has found this less reliable. Poste Restante letters need to be addressed to Poste Restante first, then your surname followed by Christian name, and finally the address of your chosen post office. Poste Restante needs to be substituted with Post Lagernd in Germany and Austria, Fermo Posta in Italy and Lista de Correos in Spain. Letters and parcels are filed at the receiving post office under the first letter of the first word, which may be your surname, first name, title or any other possibility, making them difficult to track down. A passport is required for identification and some post offices may charge upon collection. Items will only be held for one month.

Mobile phones and internet connection have merged into one fast moving subject. We are grateful that Adam from www.motorhomewifi.com was willing to give up his time to help us update this section. There are three practical ways to keep in touch using digital devices, via mobile networks, WiFi or satellite internet.

Laptop and dongle.

Mobile phones can be used abroad as long as the SIM card is roaming enabled. The same is true for 3/4G enabled devices such as smart phones, tablets, USB dongles and MiFi. Call, text, and data roaming-charges vary between network providers, especially outside of EU and EEA countries. An EU directive passed in 2012 (Regulation (EU) No 531/2012) has capped the roaming charges made against EU registered SIM cards. The caps are set to be decreased in July 2014. Maximum charges from July 2013 are: Calls received maximum 7 cents decreasing to 5 cents per minute, voicemail does not incur roaming charges, outgoing calls maximum

Free internet access is available from McDonalds in the UK, France and Spain.

24 cents decreasing to 19 cents per minute. Incoming texts free, outgoing texts maximum 8 cents decreasing to 6 cents. Internet data charges are capped at 45 cents decreasing to 20 cents per megabyte.

There are network providers that specialise in roaming. Toggle Mobile offers free incoming calls in specified countries and outgoing calls start at 3 pence per minute. At the time of reprint, roaming data was 15 pence per megabyte. UK data bundles are available. Visit www.togglemobile.co.uk for the latest rates.

Network providers may send a warning by text message if your combined spending reaches the equivalent of €50 in one month. You may be asked to opt out of this protection to continue using your device. This may be an indefinite opt out with no further text warnings. Check to see if your device allows you to monitor data use. Data monitoring apps are available. You are advised to turn 'data' off when it is not required.

You can by local SIM cards whilst abroad but it is essential that your hardware is 'unlocked'. Some countries require you to be a resident or at least give a local address. Try to find a retailer that can explain the tariff options and provide you with the correct APN settings. If possible get them to help you during SIM registration.

Internet booster antennas can increase WiFi connection range.

Connecting to the internet via WiFi can be free at bars, restaurants and fast food chains such as Mc Donalds. Campsites increasingly offer WiFi hotspots and unsecured networks are often accessible but the strength of signal may be inadequate when you are using a device inside your motorhome. A WiFi booster can greatly improve the strength of the signal. Plug and play booster antennas are available from www.motorhomewifi.com.

Directional panel antenna for WiFi connection. Photo: www.motorhomewifi.com

You have the choice of omni directional antennas or line-of-sight directional panels. Omni antennas pick up signals from all directions thus are the easiest to use. Suction cup mountings enable you to temporally stick the booster to the side of your motorhome. Caution should be used when connecting to unsecured signals since you may not be able to identify the source or the legality of using someone else's connection. Becoming part of a WiFi community will further increase your likelihood of finding a connection. FON www.fon.com is the largest of such and BT Broadband subscribers are likely to be registered by default.

Internet connection via satellites is possible and works in much the same as satellite TV and one dish can be used to do both jobs. The main advantage of internet via satellite is that it offers the most effective and reliable service throughout Europe because it is not reliant on WiFi or 3/4G signals. Unfortunately, this comes at a cost both for the receiving equipment, starting at £1,700, and the high data charges. Access is charged on a per day and download speed basis, so the more days you pre-pay for and the slower the download rate, the cheaper the daily charge. Days must be used within one or two years depending on your chosen plan. The satellite footprint does not cover eastern Europe and most of Scandinavia, although it does work in Denmark, Iceland, and Scotland. As with most things electrical, contact Road Pro or Conrad Anderson for further information and current prices.

Once you have connected to the internet you can communicate by sending emails, using social media sites or updating a blog, all of which are free to use. Internet video calls are also free through VoIP (Voice over Internet Protocol) an internet-based telephone service. There may be small annual subscription charges for membership and voicemail. In addition you can buy subscriptions that allow you to call landlines around the world for free. If you choose to subscribe to a telephone number, anyone can call you at standard rate. Calls to landlines and mobile phones are from 1.2-15 pence per minute. We use a VoIP service through Skype, www.skype.com and have successfully used it abroad when we have accessed the internet through our laptop. Several other companies including BT, www.BT.com also offer VoIP.

If Things Go Wrong

Before you travel visit the Foreign and Commonwealth Office website (www.gov.uk/fco, Tel: 0845 8502829) to check their advice about the countries you intend to visit. Travelling to countries identified as not recommended should be avoided. People touring should aim to view this website regularly to ensure they do not end up driving into an unexpected local situation.

112 is an EU-wide phone number that connects you to the police, ambulance or fire brigade, multilingual operators are often employed. The 112 number is free of charge and no roaming charges apply. If you need assistance abroad, you should contact your nearest embassy. A list of British embassies can be found at www.gov.uk/government/world, or by calling the Consular Assistance team in London (Tel: 0044 (0)20 70081500. This phone number is open 24hrs a day). The embassy can: issue replacement passports, provide assistance if you are a victim of crime, or if you are hospitalised, can provide details of lawyers, doctors, interpreters and funeral directors, contact your friends and family and help by liaising with your medical insurance company. The embassy will not: pay for or provide medical treatment, interfere with criminal or civil court proceedings, get you out of prison, investigate crimes, search for missing people, or interfere in another country's immigration policy if you do not have a visa or your passport is invalid.

Your embassy, or other authorities, may require documentation from you that may no longer be accessible to you. We strongly recommend that you ask someone that you trust to become your HQ (Headquarters) to manage your affairs, receive your mail and be on the end of the phone if you need anything. Provide them with electronic copies and colour photocopies of all your important documents, which should be kept flat in a folder in case they need to be faxed. Insurance companies should be given the name of the person who you wish to act on your behalf. We also recommend that you take copies with you or store them securely online. Copies of the documents listed below are to be kept by HQ and the originals in the motorhome safe:

- A colour photocopy of passports and the original birth certificate of each passenger to be left with HQ. In the event of passports being lost, these documents are required by the British Consulate.
- Copies of your European Health Insurance Card and medical insurance. Details of your blood group, vaccinations, any medical conditions and copies of any prescriptions.
- Copies of all documentation regarding the ownership of your vehicle, MOTs, breakdown recovery and insurance. Include copies of relevant driving licences.
- Banking details so that money can be transferred to you if necessary. Ideally leave some money with HQ to cover any expenses and some for contingencies.
- Leave a copy of next of kin details and phone numbers of anyone you may need to contact while you are away, for instance your alarm fitters, warranties, motorhome dealer, etc.
- Consider leaving copies, or locations, of wills and power of attorney documents.
- Your planned route and the countries you intend to visit.

Boaters will be familiar with the concept of a grab bag. These contain equipment needed when abandoning ship. The motorhomer's grab bag should have a photocopy of all vital documents: passports, health and vehicle documents with emergency phone numbers, a small amount of cash, and a few days worth of any medication you may need. Store important phone numbers in your mobile phone such as emergency medical helpline, travel insurance, and vehicle recovery and insurance companies. Putting a paper copy of these numbers in your purse or wallet is also advisable. When engaging in sport, such as walking, cycling, or skiing, carry your EHIC cards and a copy of your travel insurance.

Personal GPS tracking devices and mobile phones can relay your position to selected people or organisations such as the emergency services and even your Facebook or Twitter account. The Spot Satellite Messenger is a personal GPS tracking device. It has a help request button that sends a message to a designated mobile phone number, and an SOS button to relay your location to the emergency services. There is an option to send

GPS coordinates to 10 contacts, and it can place your location on Google maps so friends can log in and view your journey, visit www.findmespot.eu/en.

Jean Sear and her husband were involved in a road accident when he fainted at the wheel of their 21ft Elddis Voyager on the A9 in France. The motorhome drifted into a concrete bollard at 50mph. Both Jean and her husband survived the crash, but their insurance company declared their motorhome a write-off. Jean offers the following advice:

- Swap details with other people involved in the accident, and take many photos and video of the scene and people around you.
- You will need your EHIC and travel insurance documents if taken to hospital.
- If the hospital gives you verbal advice about what not to do as a result of your injuries (driving for example), get it in writing so that you can use it as evidence when you make a claim.
- If medical staff have advised you not to drive inform the insurance company to organise the repatriation of your motorhome.
- Contact your insurers as soon as possible and get a reference number and a free-phone number in case you need to phone again.
- Keep track of your motorhome's location. At some point you will need to visit it to obtain documentation and belongings.
- Check the amount your insurers will pay for B&B. You may choose to spend more.
- Record in a notebook the name of everyone you speak to, as well as the date and time of the conversation. Verbal agreements must be confirmed in writing. Keep every original receipt, regardless of whether the item is 'excluded' from the insurance policy.
- There is a time limit for the submission of a claim, ask what this is and stick to it.
- Keep in phone contact with your insurer throughout.

Defensive driving should be practiced at all times. Knowing the local road rules as well as observing road signs will prevent you making driving errors. Modern motorhomes are capable of being driven at normal road speeds, despite this most motorhomers drive their motorhomes slower than the rest of the traffic. This in theory sounds safer but, in practice, impatient motorists take unnecessary risks trying to overtake slow vehicles. If you wish to drive slower than the normal road speed, consider choosing quieter minor roads. Remember to pull over frequently to let vehicles behind get on their way. Driving with dipped headlights during daytime makes the vehicle more visible and has had a significant impact in reducing accidents in countries where it is compulsory. Although the Highway Code describes flashing fellow motorists as a warning, being flashed in the UK usually means a motorist is giving way or letting you out at a junction; on the continent flashing is definitely intended as a warning. Never pull out in front of a vehicle that flashes you as it is probably travelling at great speed and is not going to give way under any circumstances.

Snow ploughs keep main routes open. Photo: Andy Glasgow.

Try to avoid driving in the dark on unfamiliar roads. A-Class motorhomes offer excellent daytime visibility, but at night, reflections on the glass can be quite hard to see through, this is compounded the further you are away from the windscreen. Add rain, condensation or mist and you will have to concentrate very hard to see the road. Pedestrians may use the hard shoulder as a footpath; this is especially common in eastern Europe and Morocco. On unlit roads, it appears obligatory for pedestrians to wear black. Scooters, farm, and horse-drawn vehicles may be travelling against the traffic flow. Not all countries have effective road drainage and rain leads to flash flooding and minor landslips. Driving through deep puddles is stressful and in most cases avoidable if you wait for the rain to pass. All countries endeavour to keep the main routes open during winter with grit and snow ploughs, although snow chains may still be required. Minor roads may not have snow cleared at all. Ensure you are prepared for every eventuality if you deviate off the main routes or there is any possibility of a navigation error. Avoid driving into large cities where possible, as they can be busy, confusing and stressful experiences. Is it really worth the double parking of Rome and the chaos of Athens when you can park outside the town and use public transport to get in?

Some unscrupulous people see foreigners and foreign vehicles as an opportunity to make a quick buck. Criminals normally use distraction techniques to gain entry into your motorhome or relieve you of your wallet, handbag, or cash. We strongly recommend that you watch as many programs of BBCs 'The Real Hustle' as you can because the scams always use similar techniques, and once you learn to recognise them you stop being a vulnerable 'mark'. Clips from the shows are available at www.bbc.co.uk. We have previously written that motorway service and rest areas in southern France and Spain are the most likely place to be broken into. The same area, especially the main coast route, is the most common place for the following distraction scams to take place. One scam has smartly dressed people in a reasonable car frantically waving and pointing at the rear of the motorhome. Having encouraged the driver to stop they pull in behind and get out to identify the fault. A lit oily rag is thrown under the motorhome, the smoke and commotion is intended to get the occupants out of the motorhome, so a companion can rob valuables or steal the motorhome. The only advice that can be given is if you think it's a trick, it probably is, so making it obvious that you're not an easy target is your best defence. You should always travel with all doors and windows locked. The smell of hot brakes or burning rubber is very obvious, check mirrors, look out of the windows, see if other motorists are looking at you strangely, and switch on your rear view camera if fitted. Give the suspects the international OK sign and beckon them to go on their way. Filming or photographing them, and making it obvious will probably encourage them on their way. Remember, most mobiles now have cameras so any small object will look convincing. If you do decide you need to stop pull into a service station and stop outside the shop or restaurant, or in view of a CC TV camera. Try not to pull over until they, and any other suspect cars, are well away. Exit the vehicle calmly and lock doors before proceeding to investigate the problem.

At tourist sites, you may be asked to pay security/parking by an unsavoury character or child. This is normal in Morocco, but is likely to be a scam in the rest of Europe. Presumably you are paying them not to damage your vehicle. It is up to you whether you pay or take the risk. Just try not to let it ruin your visit, and report it if possible. This has only happened to us in Sicily at the Valley of the Temples. Should you ever be asked by official-looking people to have your money checked, 'as there has been a spate of forgeries', don't fall for it. Simply say you will call in at the police station.

Before picking up a hitchhiker, consider the dangers associated with inviting a stranger into your motorhome. Will they harm you, damage any property, invite themselves for lunch, or decide that they like travelling by motorhome and do not want to leave, especially if you have a spare bed. You may end up transporting illegal immigrants especially if you intend to cross a border.

> Handbags are like gift wrapped presents to thieves and handbag theft is the most common crime reported to Vicarious Books. Just in case this needs spelling out 'do not take a handbag with you'.

Personal security is very important when you are out and about. Always present yourself as an unsuitable victim. Handbags are like gift wrapped presents to thieves and handbag theft is the most common crime reported to Vicarious Books. Just in case this needs spelling out 'do not take a handbag with you'. Although only a very small percentage of our customers are involved in this type of crime, we advise that you keep all valuables and documentation locked in a safe within the motorhome or, when passports are required as ID, in a money pouch under clothing. If you cannot live without your handbag, ensure it can be securely closed, place the strap over your head and across your body so that you can keep the bag in front of you. Do not take or wear expensive jewellery unless you are prepared to lose it. If handbags are Christmas presents for criminals then rucksacks and bum-bags are birthday presents, if you must take one avoid carrying valuables in them.

A money belt is the only way to keep cash and cards safe when in crowded places, as long as you keep it under clothing. Usually money belts are flesh-coloured lightweight cloth belts with a zipped pocket. They are very discreet when worn around the waist and we recommend that you put it down the front of your trousers under your belt. When out and about keep most of your cash along with passports, and cards in the money belt and use a mugger's wallet for every day purchases. A mugger's wallet is a sacrificial wallet or purse that you keep in a zipped pocket. Make it look as real as possible by putting in some expired or cancelled cards, a photo, some receipts, business cards, and enough cash to get you through the day. Always use this wallet otherwise it will not be convincing, but especially at vulnerable places such as public transport or tourist attraction kiosks. If someone attempts to mug or pickpocket you they have something to steal that you are prepared to lose, hopefully it will be over quickly and no harm done.

Capital cities, large towns, and busy tourist sites are the most likely places to be followed then mugged or pick-pocketed. Always be aware of your situation, especially people brushing up against you, or engaging you in conversation, asking directions, for change or a light. If you feel someone is in your personal space, step away and don't feel embarrassed about offending them. If you think you are being followed, stick to populated areas, vary your walking pace, and stop to look in shop windows. Try to deter your follower, get them in front of you, and if necessary go into a café or get into a taxi. A useful trick if you lose each other or you are alerting your partner to a concern you may have is to decide on a code whistle or song, which is used only for these occasions. This can be a little embarrassing at first, we always use it in the supermarket, not because we feel we are going to be robbed, but somebody always wanders off. Carrying pepper spray or a baton can be tempting, but the problem with weapons is, they could be used against you, as well as the legal implications. All types of travel incur some risk. Remember motorhome related crime is rare and pickpocketing and handbag snatching are avoidable.

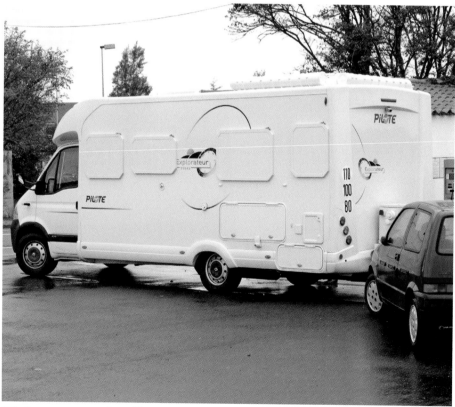

Window covers may be taking security too seriously.

Vicarious Books

Sea View Camping AND Camping Morocco

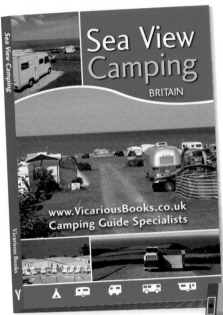

This unique campsite guide shows you all the sea view campsites around Great Britain. All you have to do is choose where you want to go and be ready for a fantastic time as you explore one of the most diverse coastlines in the world.

If you love being by the sea then this is the campsite guide for you.

only **£11.99**
inc UK P&P

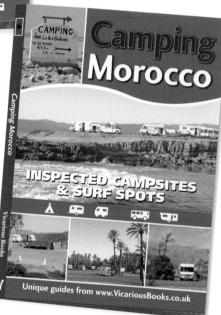

This is a campsite guide for everyone, all the sites are open all year and accessible by any form of transport. In addition to the 100 campsites, a further 50 Off-Site-Parking places have also been inspected. This is the most comprehensive and up to date campsite guide available for Morocco.

only **£12.99**
inc UK P&P

To order, give us a call or visit our website to buy online.

0131 208 3333   www.Vicarious-Shop.com

CHAPTER 6 – Where To Stay

Motorhomers travelling in Europe have hundreds of thousands of places to stop overnight, from a roadside lay-by, to a motorhome only parking area to an all-singing, all-dancing campsite. Only motorhomers have this freedom and freedom is the essence of motorhoming.

Campsites

Campsites may also be called caravan sites, campgrounds, touring parks, or campings. Despite the confusion of names most sites will accommodate tents, caravans, and motorhomes. There are over 30,000 campsites across Europe, enough to stay at a different one every night for the next 82 years. One third, 10,500, of all European campsites are located in France. Campsites range from huge five star holiday complexes to tiny campsites offering basic, affordable camping.

Small campsites often referred to as 'Mini Camping' range from gardens to farms or municipally-provided camping areas. Most have the bare necessities of water collection and disposal, and are similar to Certified

The directions said: just follow the camping signs.

Sites/Locations administered by the clubs in the UK. Pitch fees range from €5-€10 per night. Farm camping is popular in France and has a supporting scheme called 'Bienvenue à la Ferme', www.bienvenue-a-la-ferme.com. French 'Aire Naturelle' campsites are similar to UK Certified Locations/Sites, but are open only for the summer. Holland, Denmark and Germany have plenty of small, rural campsites often connected to farms or restaurants.

Trees create shade but low branches can impede large motorhomes. Lech Camping, Bavaria.

Large, privately-run campsites are common in Europe, and these have similar facilities to the large commercial campsites found in the UK. They are likely to have the following facilities: swimming pools, bars, restaurants, onsite activities, laundries, and multiple toilet blocks. British caravanners that have become accustomed to The Caravan Club's wardenised, manicured campsites will be disappointed when they go abroad. Pitches in southern Europe are devoid of grass and are normally surfaced with fine gravel or sand. The reasonable fire gap maintained between units on UK campsites is not a standard in Europe and no space is wasted. Trees normally delimit the pitches and they provide useful shade in August, conversely they make pitches dark, cold, and undesirable during winter. Trees and sunshades also create vehicle navigation obstacles and tight turns, which may be a problem if you have a large or tall motorhome. Pitch allocation can become a chaotic situation out of peak season if the campsite becomes self-regulated by the campers.

The majority of European campsites cater for caravans pitched for the season, often at the expense of touring pitches. Construction starts in March when season pitch users heave huge twin-axle caravans onto pitches, except in Italy where small, ancient caravans are pitched. Then the awning is erected and possibly a gazebo and a tarp to fill in the gaps. This tented space is carpeted or decked and a removal van load of stuff is

Home from home.

squeezed in. It really does include the kitchen sink, fridge freezer, kettle, oven, TV, and lounge furniture. Any remaining outside space is claimed and maintained by a white picket fence. Then a second removal van load of garden equipment is delivered including decking, rolls of turf, streetlights, BBQ, and all sorts of unnecessary stuff. These pitches are disassembled in September and October in some campsites, whilst others stay up for years making sections of the campsite resemble shantytowns.

Summer-only campsites normally open at Easter and close at the end of September. French campsites may not open until May and close the second week of September. Booking pitches in advance is not necessary for most European campsites except in high season, which includes bank/school holidays, and the last week in July until the third week in August. Even then, some campsites retain touring pitches or squeeze you in somewhere. July is high season in Scandinavia and popular winter campsites in Spain and Portugal have a second high season from December to February. Ski resorts across Europe have campsites that are open throughout the ski season.

Long stay pitches can really add to the ambiance.

Campsite pitch fees vary depending on the season, location and facilities, but expect to pay €20-€30 per night. There is no guarantee that expensive campsites are better than the cheap ones, or that higher star ratings relate to a better environment. Many campsites itemise their bills, for example: motorhome (small, medium, and large),

Ski resorts often have campsites that stay open all year. Photo Camping Punt Muragi, Switzerland by Andy Glasgow.

awning, car, trailer, moped, person, children, pets, electricity (priced in a 3A, 6A and 16A scale), and supplements per person for environment and tourist tax. You may also have to pay extra to use the swimming pool, tennis courts, showers, hot water and have to supply your own toilet paper! These costs can add up and can make what appears to be a cheap campsite expensive. Normally pitches have to be vacated by 10am and booking in starts from 2pm, departing late or arriving early can incur additional fees.

Campsites may offer a discount for long stays and campsite chains may offer loyalty schemes. Three companies offer Europe-wide low season discount camping schemes that generally exclude the last two weeks of July and the first three weeks of August. All three schemes offer fixed-price camping based on two people per night, including their camping unit, electricity, and a pet if taken and the campsite accepts them. Additional charges for local taxes such as tourist or environmental may apply. No booking is necessary, if you wish to advance book and want to use a discount scheme, you must make this clear at the time of booking.

LA JOURNÉE DE CAMPING EST COMPRISE DE MIDI A MIDI The day of campsite is : 12h since 12h		SAISON	HORS SAISON
ADULTE / Adult		2 60	2 10
ENFANT (-12 ans) / Children (-12 years)		1 45	1 15
EMPLACEMENT / Emplacement		4 50	3 40
BRANCHEMENT ELECTRIQUE (15 amp) Electricity 15 Amp		2 35	2 35
GARAGE MORT 1er/7ème jour / Permanent hard caravan			1 90
à partir du 8 ème / the 8e Day			3 05
TAXE SEJOUR / Tourist tax			
ADULTE / Adult		0 20	
Enfant (0-4 ans) Children (0 4 years)			
Enfant (4 - 10 ans) Children (4-10 years)		0 10	

Campsite fees may be itemised.

Touring Cheque and Camping Cheque, sell pre-paid, time bound vouchers that can be redeemed at participating campsites. These cheques are ideal if you know exactly which participating campsite you are going to and for how long. In 2013, Touring Cheque had 125 participating campsites and Camping Cheques had 629 spread thinly all over Europe. This represents a problem for people on tour unless you are prepared to drive a long way to a participating campsite. Touring Cheques, www.touringcheque.co.uk, Tel: 08448 444111, cost £13.50 and Camping Cheques, Tel: 01580 214002 www.campingcheque.co.uk, cost €15 each (per night). Cheques are in either paper form or electronic format stored on a Silver or Gold Camping Cheque card. Some campsites offer additional discounts including seven nights for six cheques, three weeks for 14 cheques or 60 nights for 30 cheques. Camping Cheques are accepted at a few campsites during July and August. Check the small print in the back of the Camping Cheque sites guide as it may be possible to return cheques for replacement immediately after they expire.

> *We purchased 30 Camping Cheques in 2003, planning to use them on our year-long tour of Europe. When we returned in 2004, we still had 10 cheques left despite going out of our way to use them. We found the campsites were in the wrong locations for us or when we turned up found that it was cheaper to pay cash, or we stayed on campsites that offered four nights for three cheques. Over the next six years, we managed to use a few, and sent expired cheques back to Camping Cheque for replacement. Each time we sent the cheques back one was taken for administration. This continued until February 2010 when despite returning the expired cheques to Camping Cheque they failed to return any cheques to us. We were not bothered by this because we had learnt that we are never in the right place at the right time to use them.*

The ACSI CampingCard is the largest discount camping scheme and has four times more participating campsites than Camping Cheque. The ACSI CampingCard is valid for one calendar year from the beginning of January until the end of December and is published just in time, on the second week of December. To obtain the card you must purchase the ACSI CampingCard guidebook listing the participating campsites. The card presses out of the front cover and in the back cover there is a map showing the sites. There is no membership, upfront fees or further administration apart from writing your own name and address on the back of the card. If you do not use the scheme it has only cost you the price of a guidebook.

Users present the card at reception of the participating campsites and pay the receptionists either €12, €14 or €16 per night, as identified in the guidebook. Some campsites offer free nights, for example stay seven and pay for six. The ACSI Camping Card is available from Vicarious Books, www.vicarious-shop.com, Tel: 0131 208 3333.

Quickstop Birkelt

Check in after 16:00 hrs
Check out before 10:00 hrs
Check in @ Reception or Restaurant
½ price campsite + full price ecotax
No free swimming pool
No Animation

A Quick Stop campsite at Larochette, Luxembourg.

Quick Stop camping is offered at selected campsites in some countries, particularly Denmark, Italy and Luxembourg. Motorhomers who arrive after 4pm and leave before 10am pay a reduced fee. The tourist office usually has details of Quick Stop campsites. There is a similar scheme operating in Spain called Formula Camper Andalusia, www.formulacamperandalucia.com. Use of the facilities is often restricted to the bare necessities. When booking in ensure that the receptionist has written down that you are paying the 'Quick Stop' price except in Italy where it is called 'Camper Stop'.

Choosing a campsite remotely can be a difficult task. When available use guidebooks that send inspectors to the campsites. Some websites allow customer comment, although you will have to learn how to interpret the comments. We have already explained that freedom is the essence of motorhoming, so instead of choosing a campsite and then fitting a holiday around it, why not decide what you want to do and then find campsites near to or suitable for the activity? Avoid advanced booking except in high season, or possibly for your first night away to give you reassurance. Obtain country-specific guidebooks when you intend to travel in just one or two countries, see the country guides on www.go-motorhoming.co.uk. When you are touring the whole of Europe the ACSI DVD is priceless, as long as you have a computer to run it on. The ACSI DVD is a searchable database of nearly 9,000 campsites that you load onto your computer, thus no internet connection is needed to search the data. Every campsite is inspected every year so the information is reliable. The Caravan Club Europe guides are popular paperback books that cover the whole of

Europe. The information is customer submitted and can be upto five years old. Vicarious Books stocks the guides mentioned above and numerous campsite guides for countries across Europe, for a complete product list visit www.vicarious-shop.com, Tel: 0131 2083333. Despite careful planning, you may arrive at your intended campsite only to find that you do not like it. Do not stay for the sake of it, as there are plenty of other places to stay, just move on.

Looking around a campsite before booking in is common practice in Europe and no one will be offended if you choose not to stay. Park near the entrance without obstructing it, enquire about price, and let reception know that you want to walk, or if it is big, drive around the site. Once you get used to being your own campsite inspector you quickly notice the important things. Out of season many of the facilities will be shut. It is not uncommon for the restaurant to be closed, the swimming pool to be drained in early September regardless of the weather, and the facilities may not be clean. A dirty campsite with limited facilities can feel very expensive. The chances are you will be allowed to select your own pitch and this can be more difficult than it appears when you consider satellite reception, hours of sunlight, noise, pitch gradient, and distance to facilities including water point and electric hook-up. Once you have chosen your pitch, return

You may need a long electricity cable.

to reception to confirm the pitch location. Enroute to your pitch, fill up with water and empty the waste tanks if necessary. Set up on your pitch, level the camper, plug in to electricity checking polarity, turn on gas, and switch the fridge over from 12V to either gas or mains electricity.

You may think as a paying guest that providing level pitches is essential; strangely, many campsite owners do not consider it important. When stopping overnight it is not worth the effort rectifying a slight lean as long as you can sleep with your feet downhill and head uphill. We carry two levelling chocks and rarely use them, but if you intend to predominantly use campsites then consider taking three or even four chocks. A simple, small two-way spirit level will give you an idea of how level the motorhome is as you jiggle around on the chosen spot. Invest in a chopping board with a drip edge to contain liquids when preparing food and ensure your plates have a raised edge, especially if you like gravy on your meal and not on your soft furnishings.

There are unwritten rules and etiquette that need to be followed at campsites to ensure you get on with your fellow campers and have a pleasant stay. Do not become a space-invader; people do not appreciate you cutting through the pitch they are paying for just because it is the quickest way to the toilet block. Having

Savaspace campsite pitch reservation sign.

used the washing-up sinks, wipe around the area and remove any food from the plug hole. After showering, mop up any water residue, soap and powder. Be aware of your noise; you may like the tune on the radio but your neighbours might not. Marking your pitch whilst you go out for the day is common on campsites where customers are allowed to choose their own pitch. Tables and chairs are commonly left on pitch and some people use small signs such as those available from Savaspace (www.savaspace.co.uk, Tel: 07801 473047).

Some campsites, mainly in France, insist that swimming trunks, not shorts, are worn in swimming pools. Some Italian campsites insist on swimmers wearing hats. Charcoal barbecues are predominantly banned on continental campsites. Some campsites prohibit the use of air conditioners and most ban generators.

Everyone looks cool around the pool in Italy.

Shower cubicles are often devoid of clothes hooks so people hang their clothes and towels over the top of the door. A bathrobe or dressing gown with a pocket for keys is useful. Even the best-maintained showers blocks look unclean after the morning and early evening rush hours, so it is worth taking some shower shoes with you. Any lightweight waterproof shoe or sandal will do as long as they prevent you coming in contact with the floor. Be warned, cheap flip-flops fling mud and dust up your damp legs as you walk back to your pitch. Very few campsite sinks have plugs so you will need to have a universal plug in your wash kit.

Laundry day creates a small problem for motorhomers on tour because washing must not be strung up at Motorhome Stopovers or when Offsite-Parking as this constitutes camping and is forbidden. Whilst launderettes are available on the continent, they can be difficult to find or park near. Self-service launderettes are beginning to appear in France at larger supermarket car parks. Most campsites have some sort of laundry system, from a service wash to hand washing sinks and some have free hot water. Campsite washing machines are convenient to use, but are rarely cheap.

Some campsites provide clothes spinners free of charge, using these significantly reduces drying times. If you intend to spend the majority of your time on a campsite with electricity you may wish to buy a mini electric washing machine. These are available from Towsure (www.towsure.co.uk, Tel: 01142 503000) and other camping shops.

French supermarkets may have self-service launderettes.

Hand-turned worktop washing machines are available in Germany and we had a Wonder Wash when we were Full-Timing. Our Wonder Wash actually washed clothes and bedding well, and was fun to use. We especially liked that it was lightweight, cost-effective and could be used anywhere, water supply permitting. Perhaps the simplest and cheapest washing option is to acquire a large lidded bucket. Before you drive, load the bucket with washing, hot water and detergent and seal the lid. When you reach your destination the magic will have happened and your clothes will be clean, subject to rinsing. Line drying is quick and easy in warm climates, but it is worth packing items made from quick drying fabrics. During the summer there is no point packing two sets of bedding, just wash on a warm day. Few campsites forbid on pitch line drying and those that do normally provide a drying area. When offsite, or on inclement days, it is possible to use the motorhome bathroom as a drying room by opening the top vent and hanging clothes from the vent on clothes hangers, a carousel is ideal for smalls and swimming costumes. When electricity is available, open the bathroom door and aim a fan heater in.

Campsites are a great place to spring clean your motorhome, as everything can be placed outside during cleaning. People partial to crusty bread will soon discover that it is a motorhome nightmare. When cutting a French baguette crusty shards fire around the motorhome fixing in upholstery, curtains and bedding. Hence, many motorhomers opt to cut bread outside. Cleaning a vehicle inside and out is the surest way to find any wear and

Spring cleaning the motorhome. Photo Andy Glasgow.

tear. Bored campers are sure to help you when you undertake repairs; they may also lend you tools and are sure to give you lots of 'useful' advice. There are plenty of accessory shops and garages across Europe should you need help or spares. French and German leisure vehicle dealers often have Motorhome Stopovers adjacent, so you can order and wait for spares and repairs. Repair jobs in Scandinavia are very expensive. If you think you are going to change your own oil check the sump plug before departing, as many cannot be undone with a spanner, but need a key. There are few camping shops or motorhome dealers in Greece so you may have to think around an issue. Water pumps, for instance, can be obtained from a boat or marine shop. *The Motorcaravan Manual* written by John Wickersham and published by Haynes is an essential guide for potential and current motorhome owners. The book discusses motorhome maintenance, including fixtures and fittings, gas, water and electric systems. We recommend taking a copy if you are intending to undertake a long trip. You can buy a copy from Vicarious Books.

Naturist campsites, large and small, are located all across Europe. These sites are often in fantastic, secluded and relaxing locations. You do not have to make a lifestyle choice to become a 'holiday naturist' and the experience is quite liberating. The continentals are a lot more relaxed about naturism and it is possible to book into a naturist campsite without needing to be a member of a registered naturist organisation. Some campsites expect you to have a photographic naturist membership card, but some campsites issue temporary identification cards if you provide passport photos. Smaller naturist sites offer a rally-like feel and may organise communal meals and group activities. Naturism has a few simple rules, you do not have to be naked all the time, sometimes it is too cold, or you have had enough sun or you are leaving the campsite. Generally nudism is only compulsory around the pool. You do have to be respectful of other people, no laughing, pointing or photos, unless you ask them to smile for the camera first. Contact British Naturism on www.british-naturism.org.uk for more details.

Most campsites have small print in their terms and conditions stating they are not liable for items damaged or stolen from the campsite. Although thefts from campsites are rare, we receive reports of thefts from campsites every year. We recommend that you follow the same precautions as you would when Offsite-Parking, always lock up properly when leaving your pitch and do not leave anything unattended that you are not prepared to lose.

Designated motorhome parking in Plouarzel, France.

Motorhome Stopovers

Dedicated motorhome parking areas are provided in many European countries and these bring welcome tourists into major and undiscovered areas alike. Motorhomers have over 8,000 Motorhome Stopovers to choose from, and as so many of them are free it would be possible to tour Europe and never pay for camping or parking. Throughout this book, we have referred to them as Motorhome Stopovers because overnight parking is normally allowed. Most Motorhome Stopovers also have a Service Point for water collection and disposal, and there are some service areas without parking. Motorhome Stopovers in rural locations normally offer free overnight parking and may charge €2-€3 for water. Motorhome Stopovers near the sea and at popular tourist destinations normally charge between €5-€20 for parking and may charge for water as well.

Motorhome Stopovers have a different name in every language:
• Aires de Service/Stationment Camping Car – France and Belgium.
• Wohnmobil-Stellplätze – Germany, Austria, and Switzerland.
• Aree di Sosta – Italy.
• Bobil – Norway.
• Area de Servicio para Autocaravanas – Spain and Portugal.

Motorhome Stopovers had no established name in English until Vicarious Books published the 'All the Aires' series of guidebooks. Aires is a shortened version of the French term Aire de Services but even this is better described as

Motorhome Stopovers, like this one at Thann, allow motorhomers to come and go as they please.

serviced Motorhome Stopovers. To avoid confusion the term Motorhome Stopover is used throughout this book except when discussing Motorhome Stopovers in specific countries, when the local term is sometimes used.

There is some confusion about motorway parking, especially in France where the motorway service stations are also referred to as Aires. The word 'aire' in French means 'area' and is used for lots of things. Anyone can stop at a motorway service station but we receive more reports of theft at motorway service stations than any other place, especially in southern France and Spain. Local traffic police on the AP7 in Spain confirmed that vehicles, including motorhomes and trucks, were being broken into on that motorway. They believed it was a national problem on the Spanish motorway network. Therefore we would never recommend that you park overnight at motorway service stations, even if they have a Service Point and what appears to be suitable parking.

Aire simply means Area, and this sign refers to motorway parking. Motorhome Stopovers are occasionally signed 'Aire Camping-Car' but are usually indicated with a motorhome symbol.

Motorway parking areas may look suitable but these are anonymous places and motorhomers should never park overnight on them.

NORMAS DE UTILIZACIÓN DEL ÁREA PARA AUTOCARAVANAS

El estacionamiento máximo será de 48 horas.
- Queda prohibido sacar de la autocaravana cualquier elemento como sillas,mesas,barbacoas, toldo, tendal, etc... ya que esto es considerado como "acampada" y las leyes prohíben expresamente la acampada libre.
- El área debe de mantenerse en perfecto estado de limpieza.
- Cuando se use el borne de llenado y vaciado, no derramar líquidos fuera de la pileta y rejilla dejando todo limpio.
-"El punto de vaciado del WC está situado sobre la acera junto a las plazas de aparcamiento de disminuidos físicos"

RULES FOR THE CAMPERVAN AREA

Maximum parking 48 hours.
- Taking oug things such as chairs,tables, barbecues,awnings, etc... and hanging out clothes is FORBIDDEN because that is considered "camping" by   laws which expressly ban free camping.
- The area must be kept in perfect cleaning condition.
- When using the filling and emptying terminal, be careful not to spill liquids outside the sink and grille and leave everithing clean.
-"The point of emptying of theWC, is placed in the sidewalk, close to the parking for disable persons"

The law does not allow for camping equipment to be used at Motorhome Stopovers.

Municipally provided Motorhome Stopovers normally look like any other municipal parking area and you are free to come and go as you please. Guardians are only present at a small number of commercial Motorhome Stopovers so apart from at these there is no way of reserving a space. After your day out you should plan to visit two or three Motorhome Stopovers on route to your next chosen activity. If your first choice is full or unsuitable, move on to the next. You may be worried about using one for the first time. On your first attempt, visit in daylight to get a feel for them. On arrival, park, put the kettle on, and have a nice cup of tea. Look at the facilities, talk to the other motorhomers, and then look around the local area. By using Motorhome Stopovers, you are likely to visit places not listed in any mainstream tourist information guidebook. When you find a relaxing or interesting place you can stay another day, if no time limit is displayed then 48 hours is the unwritten rule. You should try to spend the equivalent of campsite fees locally in the village shops and cafés, or buy some diesel from the fuel station.

Motorhomes weighing up to 3,500kg are classified as cars in mainland Europe and for safety reasons car drivers are allowed to park and rest in their vehicles. This entitlement does not allow car drivers to put up tents or set up caravans because this is deemed camping. Owners of caravans and American-style fifth wheel caravans may think this unfair but the rules are the rules and foreign tourists have no exemption. A motorhome is not deemed to be camping if it is self-sufficient, therefore the occupants can cook, eat, and sleep within a motorhome as long as they do not place anything outside. An onboard toilet is a necessity and wastewater from sinks must not be discharged onto the ground or into containers that need to be placed outside. Some irresponsible motorhomers ignore these rules, and use levelling chocks, put out tables and chairs, wind out awnings, hang up washing, run generators, and generally set up camp. Imagine how you would feel if people were doing that opposite your home, presumably you would complain to your local council and demand that they banned motorhomes from the parking area.

Whatever country you are in, and regardless of what they are called, Motorhome Stopovers exist in four main forms:

Service Points: Service Points, sometimes referred to as bornes, dump or sani stations, are areas where motorhomes can dispose of wastewater and toilet waste, refill drinking water tanks and sometimes hook-up to mains electricity. There are several manufacturers of self-contained Service Points

Flot Bleu Service Point - France.

Euro Relais Mini - France and Portugal.

Urba Flux Service Point - France.

Holiday Clean - Germany and Norway. Photo: Andy Glasgow.

and the brand names include: Flot Bleu, Euro Relais, Aire Services and Holiday Clean. Approximately half of all the Service Points found around Europe are simply custom made by a builder and consist of a tap and a grated drain.

Service Points are normally attached to a motorhome parking area, but may be on the forecourt of a fuel station. Service Points are often turned off during winter to prevent frost damage, therefore you should plan to visit several Service Points during the day and service when you find one working.

Use only water points marked as drinking water to fill your water tank, never to wash your toilet cassette. A bottle allows water refilling without the need for multiple hose adaptors.

Water: Unless there is a sign to say otherwise, it is safe to assume the water is potable, although tap hygiene is poor due to cross-contamination from toilet waste. Using disinfectant wipes or spray before drawing water from Service Points will improve hygiene. Taps vary widely, some are threaded to assist hose connection and others are too large to attach a hose. When payment is required to draw water it is normally limited to 100L.

Wastewater Disposal: Normally a drive-over metal grate is provided to facilitate the disposal of wastewater. Badly chosen materials, poor or illogical construction and careless driving often leads to their destruction. Take a length of hosepipe to direct wastewater accurately.

Never place the toilet nozzle around the tap, but leave a gap of a few centimetres to avoid cross-contamination. The next person may use that tap for their fresh water.

Toilet Waste Disposal: Always wear waterproof gauntlets during toilet emptying. Take a moment to consider where and how to empty your toilet cassette, removing any grates before emptying. Do not rush cassette emptying as spillage and splashing will occur. Glugging can be reduced by pressing the vent button on the toilet cassette during emptying. Often a water tap is located above the toilet emptying point and these tend to flow even if payment is required for other services. Never put the cassette spout over a tap that may be used for drawing drinking water. We have a

Left: Sometimes the toilet emptying point is covered by a grid.
Right: Having donned tough rubber gloves, lift the grid before emptying. This prevents solids and paper being left high and dry.

Left: Having emptied the toilet, flush the drain with your grey water or use the flushing system.
Right: Once the area is clean, replace the grid.

gallery of photographs that show toilet waste sitting high and dry on drain covers. In most cases, this is not because people have emptied the cassette in the wrong place, but it has happened as they empty the water out after rinsing and unexpected solids are discharged. Few Service Points are suitable for emptying fixed-tank toilet systems, such as those found on American RVs. We strongly recommend that you fit a macerator if your motorhome has a fixed toilet tank and travel with a long length of pipe.

Electric Hook-Up: Very few motorhome Service Points offer unlimited free electricity. Some of the professionally manufactured, self-contained Service Points require payment by coin or token before you can draw water and electricity. In this situation electricity is usually dispensed for a limited period, often one hour. The theory is that you can charge your batteries. In

This bollard provides a time-bound amount of electricity for a fee.

reality this is insufficient time and few people bother to plug in. However if you are organised you can charge all your battery-operated gadgets, blow-dry hair, boil kettles and fill flasks. Unfortunately there is rarely an external trip switch on these Service Points and, once tripped, there is no way of making the electricity work again, despite having paid for it. Sometimes, particularly in Germany, a separate coin operated electricity bollard is provided and a time-bound or metered amount of electricity is available. Some stopovers include electricity in the nightly charge, but may not have enough plug sockets for every motorhome. Stopping at a campsite is the only guaranteed way to get electricity.

Custom made Service Points are common in France.

Custom Service Points vary widely as they are produced by local craftmen.

Custom Service Points can be easy to miss.

Custom Service Points vary in useability.

Be responsible. If the Service Point is out of order, don't make the situation worse.

Free electricity is uncommon at Motorhome Stopovers; when available, sharing is expected.

Tokens And Pay Service Points:
Tokens are called 'jetons' in French. Less than one quarter of the Service Points in Europe require tokens. Payment by credit card is increasing.

Tokens are normally available from local shops, especially boulangeries (bakers), bar tabacs, tourist offices, the mairie (town hall) and campsites if adjacent. Tokens may be free, but typically cost €2-3. Information panels or signs fixed to the Service Point normally indicate where tokens are available.

French tokens:

Techno Money (TM) has a distinctive pattern on the front. It is the same size as a 10p piece.

The 3/3 token is the same both sides with 3 grooves on each. It is the same size as a 10p piece.

The front of the Euro Relais (ER) token is branded. The token is slightly bigger than a 10p piece.

The 2/1 token has one groove on the front and 2 on the back. It is the size of a 2p piece.

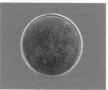

The front of the Flot Bleu token is branded and the token is the size of a £1 coin, but not as thick.

Motorhome parking is normally indicated by a sign depicting a motorhome.

Overnight Parking: Motorhome parking is mostly municipally provided, but some privately operated tourist attractions and supermarkets have a section of motorhome parking. Normally signs depicting a motorhome identify the area to be motorhome parking, although the signage does vary significantly. Sometimes designated parking areas are shared with cars and can be busy during the day, but empty at night. Motorhome Stopovers operate on a first come, first served basis and it is not possible to reserve a space. Stopping is generally limited to 48 hours unless otherwise stated, as they are designed to be used whilst touring and not for an extended holiday. Always park in designated bays, if provided, and never obstruct roadways or Service Points. Motorhome Stopovers may not have designated spaces, and it is normal to park less than a vehicle width from your neighbours. If the stopover is full find another one. 10 years ago motorhomes longer than 6m were rare, now motorhomes shorter than 6m are rare, the result is that a lot of the old parking areas are unsuitable for modern motorhomes. People with sub-6m motorhomes can take advantage of this and will find that they can stop on their own in wonderful locations. Anywhere that attracts a lot of motorhomes has had to manage the situation, and a lot of coastal towns have done this by banning motorhomes completely. Towns that have continued to accommodate motorhomes normally allow parking at specified places only, which are often barrier and parking meter controlled. To enjoy the freedom of motorhoming we recommend that you plan your travels so that you avoid the obvious places. For example, if you want to drive around the French coast expect to pay at least €5 per night; you can get around this by heading inland each evening.

Vineyards, Farms And Private Gardens: Visiting a farm or vineyard where you can watch local producers at work, then park overnight is a romantic idea. Motorhomers are invited to do just this at 4,000 farms and vineyards across Europe. These are often available only to self-sufficient motorhomes because of the parking and camping rules previously discussed. There are several membership schemes and publications to

Farm stop, Denmark. Photo: Andy Glasgow.

guide you, all of which are available from Vicarious Books. For Denmark (Nordic Camper Guide), France (France Passion), Germany (Bord Atlas), Italy (Fattore Amico), and Spain (España Discovery). Apart from Denmark and Germany, these are motorhome-only membership schemes that allow 24 hours free parking at each listing. The local producers may wish to show you their wares, although there is no obligation to buy unless you are stopping at a restaurant or bar, and you are likely to be taken on an informative and interesting tour whether or not you can converse with your host. Remember these are not campsites but people's homes and businesses, so park as if you were on a Motorhome Stopover and do not set up camp.

In most European countries the legal level of alcohol in blood/breath when driving is significantly lower than the UK, and several European countries have zero percentage tolerance to alcohol on the breath. It is recommended that no alcohol is consumed if you intend to drive. Remember that alcohol consumed the night before may still be in the system, so leave plenty of time before driving.

Motorhome Campsites: There are certain areas that are overwhelmed by motorhomes. To accommodate them, local authorities have built what can only be described as Motorhome Campsites, but are in fact sophisticated Motorhome Stopovers. Some Motorhome Campsites have been developed by entrepreneurial individuals who have manipulated planning laws by only accommodating motorhomes. European motorhomers rarely use traditional campsites. Despite this, they will pay to stop at Motorhome Campsites with reasonable prices. Motorhome Campsites differ from traditional campsites because they are mostly hardstanding, have no reception, and rarely have a sanitary block. Motorhomers seem willing to use them because they are less expensive, are open all year, and accommodate only motorhomes. Electric hook-up is often available from pay meter points, and most people hook-up if it is reasonably priced. Entry may be gained through a credit card-operated barrier system. Before entering you insert your credit or debit card, type in your vehicle registration number and the barrier opens. When you depart you insert your card and are charged accordingly. The barrier opens and you are free to leave. Ironically, a few former municipal campsites have been converted into motorhome-only campsites and as a result are used all year round.

PS : Des contrôles seront effectués.

INFORMATION CAMPING - CARS

En raison des abus de certains camping-caristes, la commune va prochainement instaurer un droit de stationnement qui s'élèvera à 5 € par nuit.

Merci de votre compréhension.

Due to abuse of some camping car owners, the town will soon establish a parking fee that will be 5 € per night.

Thank you for undertanting.

Décret du 06-02-1932

Authorities at Catillon sur Sambre reacted to abuse by charging.

Using Motorhome Stopovers is a luxury not a right, so park sympathetically to your neighbours and use the Service Point and facilities responsibly. Always abide by the RESPECT rules:

Respect the environment
Elect to use un-crowded Motorhome Stopovers
Shop locally
Park responsibly
Exercise courteous behaviour
Communicate with others
Totally abide by these rules

Service Points may have been broken by a previous visitor and may not be working.

Responsible use of Motorhome Stopovers is vital so that local communities keep them open. Use them, but don't abuse them. Common stopover abuse includes: not cleaning up the Service Point after emptying the toilet, camping on the stopover, parking over more than one bay, hanging out washing, breaking the Service Point, leaving without paying, and overstaying the time limit. It is with sadness that we have noticed the increase of these abuses over the last 10 years. Often Motorhome Stopovers are provided and funded by the local community, so make a conscious effort to repay their generosity. Remember you represent the motorhome community; being miserly, abusing facilities and other unacceptable behaviour leads to resentment and stopovers closing.

You will stumble across Motorhome Stopovers in certain areas, but they may be as rare as hens' teeth 10 miles down the road. To make the most of your trips you need to travel with the best information available. Motorhome Stopover guidebooks fall into two categories, those produced following professional inspection and those compiled from customer and tourist board submissions. When available, buy guidebooks that had professional inspectors gathering the information so that you have continuity of information. There are comprehensive stopover websites including www.eurocampingcar.com and www.campingcar.info. Read all the customer comments and make your own conclusions, also check the date of comments to ensure the information is current. Vicarious Books is a specialist stockist and publisher of Motorhome Stopover guides: visit www.vicarious-shop.com to see the product range.

Overnight stopping place in Australia.

You may wish to Offsite Park beside the sea, but in reality most beach parking has overnight parking exclusion signs.

Offsite-Parking

Parking by the side of the road for a short period to rest is legally allowed in some European countries and can sometimes, especially in Scandinavia, be your only option. This has a few names, including 'free camping' and 'wild camping', however Offsite-Parking describes it better, as that is essentially what you are doing. Scandinavia offers endless idyllic Offsite-Parking possibilities, but the opposite is true of the Mediterranean coast.

You can stay in some fantastic locations but 90 per cent of your Offsite-Parking night stops will be unglamorous car parks and lay-bys. The terms 'free/wild camping' are misleading as they suggest that you unpack and set up as if on a campsite. In countries where stopping by the side of the road is legal, camping by the side of the road is not. When Offsite-Parking the objective is to remain inconspicuous and be able to leave at a moment's notice. Always Offsite-Park considerately, trying to cause the least offence to locals. Remember Offsite-Parking is a luxury or a necessity, and should never be considered a right. This means that items should not be placed around the motorhome, such as tables, chairs and bikes, and if towing a trailer, it should remain hitched. Even if the law allows you to stop by the side of the road overnight, it does not allow you to stay there for long periods of time. You should aim to stop at teatime and depart after breakfast.

Do not camp when Offsite-Parking.

Scandinavia, with the exception of Denmark, encourages open access to its fantastic countryside and wilderness. The following phrases are often used to describe this idea: 'the freedom to roam', 'the right of public access', 'the right to roam', 'Everyman's Right'. Although described in many ways this refers to the right to walk, cycle, ride, ski and camp on any land, or swim in any water body. Historically open access was granted with walkers and canvas camping in mind and vehicles are prohibited from driving or parking off road. The scarcity of campsites in northern Scandinavia often makes Offsite-Parking the only option and the Scandinavian authorities are tolerant to this as long as you are parking on hard-standing. Taking advantage of this open access does not come without its responsibilities. The natives have great respect for their unique environments and protect them zealously. The rules are simple and must be obeyed:

- Do not disturb or destroy the environment.
- Dispose of your litter and waste only in the facilities provided.
- Private gardens and land under cultivation are exempted from open access.
- Camping or overnight parking is not permitted within 150m of a dwelling house.
- Local restrictions can apply, especially in nature reserves and in other protected areas.

Suitable parking places are hard to find in the populated southern parts of Scandinavia because of the 150m, no-camping rule around dwellings. Always respect any local instructions, otherwise Scandinavia is waiting to be discovered.

Offsite-Parking is possible across most of Europe, although not necessarily legal. We have previously written that Offsite-Parking is not really an option at popular motorhome destinations, but once away from the masses, you will have no problems if you choose wisely. The most important thing is to find somewhere that nobody has a strong feeling of ownership over, such as municipally provided parking outside sports facilities, and cemeteries often have deathly quiet parking. Bear in mind that out-of-town parking spots are often popular with local lovers or noisy youths and industrial estates become noisy around 4am. Do not park where it clearly signs not to and do not block driveways or entrances. When parking in idyllic locations try to imagine how you would feel if you had paid a premium for a house with a view and a motorhome turned up and completely blocked it.

Most nights spent Offsite-Parking will be in urban car parks.

For your safety and to ensure a restful night's sleep park in an illuminated area close enough to habitation to feel safe but far enough away to not cause offence. Always park so you can drive off at a moment's notice, face an exit and put everything away before you go to bed. Never put on external screens, use chocks or anything else that makes you exit the motorhome before you can drive off. Allow time to investigate your parking place, stop for a cup of tea or a meal and watch what and who is about. Have a walk around the area and familiarise yourself with it and have a drink (not alcoholic) in the nearest bar so locals are not suspicious of you.

Do not Offsite-Park where signs prohibit.

When parking with other motorhomers, try to talk to your neighbours so they know who should be entering your motorhome. Do not drink, as European law is tougher on drink drivers than UK law, and even one drink is too much. Once you've done all that, relax and enjoy the biggest freedom that motorhoming gives you, the ability to be at home wherever you are.

Where motorhomers are becoming a problem, the authorities may attempt to discourage them by moving them on. This is the first step before the barriers and exclusion signs go up. Being 'moved on' refers to being asked to leave by an official, often the

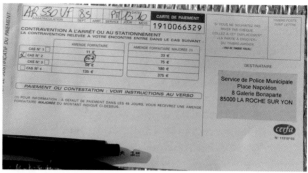

A motorhome fined for outstaying its welcome.

police. If you are 'knocked up', a knocking on the door, a common response is that you are resting or that you are only parking overnight. Ensure you have stopped somewhere that you are legally allowed to, and even if you have, do not assume that you will not be disturbed. Normally if you are knocked up by an official they will politely ask you to leave, but in the worst case scenario you may have to pay a fine. Police have fined motorhomers at popular Offsite-Parking spots in Spain and Portugal. On-the-spot fines for parking and traffic offences are common in Europe and immediate payment is expected.

Over the past 10 years we have noticed a dramatic increase in the number of height barriers and motorhome exclusion signs. The negative feelings towards motorhomers is generally created by bad motorhoming practices such as emptying wastewater tanks onto the ground, emptying toilets in any local drain regardless of its purpose, parking in huge numbers, running generators and being noisy, allowing pets to foul in the local areas, leaving

Sign indicates motorhomes are not allowed to park between 8pm and 8am.

litter, parking for the best view or closest to the beach, hanging out washing, and camping. Although your monthly budget can be reduced by Offsite-Parking, it is essential that this is done in a responsible manner and in accordance to the country's law, regardless of what other motorhomers are doing. Failing to be responsible will just lead to more motorhome exclusion signs.

CHAPTER 7 - Key Country Guides

This chapter is a motorhomer's guide to the six countries you are most likely to visit. All the other countries of Europe are detailed on www.go-motorhoming.co.uk.

France
France has something for everyone from lavender days in Provence, to awesome alpine activities, to Mediterranean meanders. During the Tour de France, it appears that every motorhome ('Camping Car' in French) in France is lining the mountain stages. There are annual race stages through the Pyrenees and Alps, but the route changes every year. You can check the stages online at www.letour.fr.

Where To Stay
France has a mind-boggling 10,400 campsites that range from tiny summer-only camping areas to large family fun parks. The star rating system applied to French

Stenay, France.

campsites is inconsistent, therefore we recommend that you walk around the campsite and check the facilities before you book in. French campsites are generally well signed from the nearest town or village, so you will not need directions to find them. Pleasant municipally run campsites are found all over France. Often they are located in small villages and normally alongside a river if there is one. The pitch fees are low and the facilities basic, but the campsites normally have a comfortable ambiance. Small rural campsites, with less than 25 pitches, are identified as Aire Naturelle in French. These small sites are often very basic but have a great appeal. Camping on farms is available through the Bienvenue à la ferme scheme, see www.bienvenue-a-la-ferme.com for details. Site entrances are clearly marked with the scheme's yellow-flower symbol. Les Castels is an organisation that promotes 40 campsites that are located in chateaux grounds, see www.camping-castels.co.uk for details. A good selection of campsites is listed at www.campingfrance.com. The French publication *Le Guide Officiel Camping Caravaning* lists 10,340 French campsites, including all the municipal and small campsites. This guide is written in French, but has an English key and is easy to use. Vicarious Books stocks this guide and it is available to buy in large French supermarkets from April, but may not be restocked once sold out.

France has 2,800 Motorhome Stopovers called 'Aires de services', or Aires for short. These are detailed in *All the Aires France,* published by Vicarious Books. This is the only French Aires guide written in English and all 2,700 Aires listed have been inspected and photographed. *Le Guide National des Aires de Services* and *Le Guide Official Aires de Services* are produced by rival French motorhome magazines. The Aires are not inspected and few have photographs. The French language Aires guides are on sale in large French supermarkets from April, but may not be restocked once sold out. Members of *France Passion* can stop overnight for free in their motorhomes at farms and vineyards all over France. Membership runs from Easter to Easter and is gained by buying the current guidebook. Host establishments vary considerably so it is a good idea to check out two or three before deciding where to stop. This scheme gives you a unique insight into French culture and the hosts are likely to show you how the goods are produced and grown, even if language prevents conversation. GPS coordinates are downloadable making remote host sites less difficult to find. All the guides mentioned above are available from Vicarious Books. Offsite-Parking is possible in France as long as it is undertaken in accordance with the traffic and parking laws.

Driving And Roads
France has twice the landmass of the UK, but has a similar number of residents. Consequently, traffic is light outside of major urban areas and there would be even less if all the motorways were free. French toll motorways are correctly named Autoroute but are normally signed and referred to as 'péage', which translates to toll in English. These well-maintained motorways are quick and quiet but expensive, and for that reason most truck and domestic drivers use the non-toll main roads called routes nationales. Driving on French Autoroutes is mind numbingly boring and it is hard to resist driving at high speeds, just to get it over with. Modern panel vans can easily drive at the 130kmh (80mph) upper speed limit and so can motorhomes if you are willing to accept the dramatically increased fuel consumption. Fuel at Autoroute service areas is 10-20 cents

per litre more than from supermarkets. Just in case you are only reading this section, for safety reasons never park overnight at Autoroute service or rest areas and maintain vigilance when you use them at any time of day. For further information about Autoroutes visit www.autoroutes.fr.

 French trunk roads are called 'routes nationales'. Often these main roads are marked red on road maps. Routes nationales are mostly single carriageway; despite this, they take the majority of traffic. The French driving style is consistent across the country. Mostly, car drivers are calm and unrushed in towns and villages, but they turn into speed-freaks on open roads. Truck drivers will maintain a speed of 90kmh (56mph) whenever possible. Due to a lack of passing places, frustrated drivers take extraordinary risks when overtaking, and being overtaken by trucks is very scary. Speeding is normal on the open road, but the 50kph (31mph) speed limit is observed in areas of habitation. In order to reduce accidents and speeding, more speed cameras are being installed, often they are not signed and may not be marked on maps. Mobile speed cameras and road checks are common at town and village boundaries. Bypasses are infrequent in France so the main routes pass through towns and villages. The majority of these main-road, built-up areas have a depressing look due to the grey film from pollution that coats the buildings. When driving past shops, be prepared for other drivers making emergency bread stops as they realise they just passed a bakery. See speed limits on page 214.

The nicest roads to drive are the lesser roads, marked yellow on *Michelin France* road atlas. These minor routes tend to accommodate local traffic only. They pass through pretty landscapes and interesting villages, where you will be able to stop without disturbance.

Unfortunately, some French drivers seem to lack forethought and appear to be unable to assess how their actions will affect other road users. Head-on collisions, on perfectly straight roads, are common in France. Drivers often maintain their speed even if there is an obstruction on the road or their vehicle is sufficiently wide to overhang the white line. On narrow lanes, be prepared to pull off the road, avoiding any ditches, to allow oncoming vehicles to pass.

Priorité à Droite (priority to the right) is a tourist's worst nightmare. Thankfully, it has been removed from most towns and villages, but you are still likely to find yourself in a situation where you have no idea who has priority. What makes this inconstancy so dangerous is that some minor roads have priority over the main route and the local drivers will join the main route at speed. You should avoid giving way to vehicles on the right when it is not appropriate, as doing so will cause all sorts of confusion, instead drive as if priority to the right exists unless road markings and signs prove otherwise. Some villages and towns have 'Priorité à Droite' signs written at the boundaries, but normally a sign displaying a yellow diamond indicates that there is no priority to the right. Cancellation signs will be displayed at village exits and normal road rules apply. Apparently, some villages are incapable of commitment and have removed all the road markings! At junctions where the priority is unclear, proceed confidently but keep an eye on every direction, French drivers are very cautious at junctions and will willingly giveway.

Priority to the right, France.

Roundabouts are a relatively new addition to French roads and help with priority issues. Most roundabouts flow the same as the UK, which may be indicated by signs saying 'Vous n'avez pas la priorité' or 'Cédez le passage'. Occasionally, in towns and villages, the priority on a roundabout will be to the right, this is of course ludicrous but no worse than putting traffic lights on roundabouts like they do in the UK. French traffic lights go from red to green skipping amber when releasing traffic. Light changes tend to be a long time apart. Crossroads controlled by traffic lights may be left on flashing amber lights outside of rush hour, this indicates that you can proceed with caution; the problem is no one knows who has priority.

Roads are commonly marked with temporary 'Route Barrée' signs (road closed) during road works or when markets are blocking the road. A deviation route is not always provided. Traffic calming chicanes and road humps are very common in towns and villages and their design ensures that you have to drive slowly over or around them to prevent damaging your vehicle.

When driving along narrow mountain lanes it is French driving etiquette to give-way to traffic travelling uphill, this includes pulling over and reversing if necessary. The French highway code requires the sounding of horns on twisting roads with reduced visibility. The *Michelin France Tourist and Motoring Atlas* highlights difficult or dangerous sections of roads. Less confident motorhome drivers should avoid these routes. High passes may be closed during winter and spring due to snow, snowdrifts, or wind. Never drive along roads signed 'Route Barrée' or 'Fermé', and never open gates that are used to close off mountain roads.

LPG availability varies from region to region but is sufficiently available across the whole country, especially on the Autoroutes. LPG stations are listed in the rear of *All the Aires France.* The following websites list LPG outlets http://stations.gpl.online.fr/appli/index.php and www.jerouleaugpl.com/installateurs.php lists Total fuel stations with LPG.

Germany

Germany has it all: bountiful beer, amazing architecture, stunning scenery and toll-free roads. History vultures will be flying high at Hitler's Eagle's Nest. Bavaria has some pivotal pilgrimage sites including the Wieskirche and octagonal Chapel of Grace with its Black Madonna. Hopeless romantics may wish to start or end their scenic drive along 'Romantische Strasse' taking in elaborate country houses and castles along the way. The Romantic Road is Germany's most popular tourist route and runs from Fussen in southern Bavaria 340km north to Wurzburg. Wine not meander alongside the Mösel or Rhine and marvel at the seemingly endless vineyards. Motorhome tourists are well catered for and can stop at any of the

Mösel valley, Germany.

frequent stellplätze along all three routes. Getting around by foot and bicycle could not be easier as the buses and ferries can transport you and your bike. Germany is crisscrossed by 7,000km of clearly signed cycle routes and there are plenty of marked walking trails as well. Germany's ski resorts are a well-kept secret. Generally the resorts are low-key, family-friendly, and affordable. Cash is king in Germany and very few places take credit or debit cards; consequently, you will have to make regular visits to cash machines.

Where To Stay

Germany has 3,500 campsites that cater for all desires and budgets. The German Tourist Board-produced guidebook *Campsites and Motorhome Sites in Germany,* is written in English, and lists 800 campsites. 1,900 German campsites are listed on http://en.camping.info/campsites.

Motorhome Stopovers are called Wohnmobil stellplätze in Germany and there are over 2,000 to choose from. German motorhomers are happy to pay for electricity and plenty of stellplätze offer hook-up. Often there will be meter-controlled hook-up bollards distributing electricity by kilowatts used or duration, commonly €2 for 12 hours. German stellplätze are the best-kept Motorhome Stopovers in Europe, making Germany a joy to visit. There are several important road signs to watch out for: 'Nur Fur' means 'only for', 'Nur Von' means 'only from' whilst 'Frei' means 'entry allowed' or 'parking spaces available'. The publication *Bord Atlas* by Reise Mobil, lists 1,564 Motorhome Stopovers and 1,131 farm and vineyard stops located in Germany. This comes as a pack of two guidebooks and is available from German bookshops and newsagents. Both the above books are available from Vicarious Books, www.vicarious-shop.com, Tel: 0131 208 3333. Offsite-parking is possible in Germany as long as it is undertaken in accordance with the traffic and parking laws.

Driving And Roads

Germany is a good driving country with only a few things to note. German driving tests are the most comprehensive in Europe and the driving style reflects this. Motorways, 'Autobahn', across Germany are toll-free and frequently have only two lanes. Regardless of this there will be very fast cars on them. Some motorways have no speed limit, except during bad weather conditions when speed limits are indicated on overhead gantries. Vehicles over 3,500kg are frequently restricted to the inside lane, so look out for signs if you are affected. Do not 'middle lane' on German motorways because it is very dangerous, and you are likely to be chastised. Before overtaking, take a good look in your mirrors, then if no speeding cars can be seen, indicate and overtake without delay. Motorway exits are signposted as 'Ausfahrt'. Be aware that very short slip lanes followed by unbelievably steep bends are common.

Cyclists often have priority at traffic lights, therefore be vigilant when turning right in towns and be prepared to stop. Winter tyres are compulsory in Germany during snow or icy conditions and snow chains are not considered to be enough. Therefore, it is advisable to have winter tyres fitted to your motorhome if you visit Germany between October and April. See www.bmv.de for detailed information about road rules. Free roadside parking may be time-bound and vehicles must display the arrival time on a time disc. Discs are available from newsagents for a few euros.

Low emission zones, called 'Umweltzonen' in Germany, are on the increase. Vehicles entering an Umweltzone must display a colour-coded sticker (red, yellow, or green) that identifies the euro emission class of the vehicle. Non-compliance can result in a €40 fine. The sticker must be stuck on the inside of the windscreen at the bottom right corner. Some towns exclude higher emission, red stickered vehicles, and over time this will increasingly include yellow stickers. The sticker is valid for the entire life of the vehicle as long as the number plate is unchanged. Umweltzone stickers cost €29.90, see www.umwelt-plakette.de. Stickers can also be issued at local Dekra vehicle registration offices for €5. www.dekra.de has a Dekra station search facility. Just type in a postcode or town name and the details of the nearest Dekra office is displayed. Red stickers are awarded to Euro 2 and Euro 1 diesel cars/motorhomes with retrofit particulate filters. Yellow stickers are awarded to Euro 3 and Euro 2 diesel cars/motorhomes with retrofit particulate filters. Green stickers are awarded to Euro 4/5 and Euro 3 diesel cars/motorhomes with retrofit particulate filters. Green stickers are also awarded to cars/motorhomes with petrol engines fitted with closed-loop catalytic converters, excluding some older models. Visit www.umwelt.nrw.de and click 'English', then 'low emissions zones' for a good explanation of how engines are given a Euro rating. Also see page 37.

LPG is widely available and a list of LPG stations is provided at www.autogastanken.de/de/tanken/autogastankstellen-karte.html. The ADAC *Reise Atlas* (1:200,000) shows LPG stations and roads that exclude cars towing caravans. The atlas is available from bookshops in Germany and is updated biannually.

Italy

Rome was not built in a day and Italy has so much to see and do it is hard to know where to start. Italy has been a firm favourite with grand tourers for centuries, and if we had only one month to travel Europe we would spend three weeks in Italy. Adventurous winter Sun-Seekers should head south to Sicily and drive around Etna, the largest volcano in Europe and one of the most active in the world. Visit www.funiviaetna.com for more information about visiting Etna.

Assisi, Italy. Photo: Andy Glasgow.

Where To Stay

Italian campsites are very expensive and you are unlikely to feel that you are getting good value for money. Poor facilities and unlevel pitches are common and you are advised to visit campsites that are in one of the discount schemes, see page 172. A database of Italian campsites is published online at www.camping.it. Look out for 'Agri Tourismo' signs, as you will often be able to park overnight for a few euros.

Italy has approximately 1,000 Motorhome Stopovers called 'Aree di Sosta' translating to area to stop. Motorhome Stopovers near tourist attractions are more like motorhome campsites; elsewhere they are located in municipal car parks and often have simple custom-built Service Points. There are few publications listing Italian stopovers. At the time of reprint Camperstop Europe was the only guide available in the UK that listed a reasonable amount of Italian stopovers. *All the Aires Mountains,* published by Vicarious Books, details campsites and Motorhome Stopovers in the mountains of northern Italy and Sicily. Guides are available at www.vicarious-shop.com. Details of Area di Sostas can be found online at www.camperonline.it. Offsite-Parking is possible in Italy as long as the traffic and parking laws are complied with. Italians have an interesting take on what remote car parks should be used for so bear this in mind when choosing overnight parking. Thankfully, the lovers tend to be quiet, but local youths will party late on Friday and Saturday nights. This can be a little alarming to start with but you soon learn to sleep through it.

Driving And Roads
Whilst travelling south down Italy you will notice that road conditions continually deteriorate the further away from the industrial north you get. Motorways tend to have tolls, see www.autostrade.it, but the minor roads that run parallel are free and are often more interesting and challenging. Roads have been renumbered over the past few years, so maps and addresses may be out of date. Cycling clubs are common and pelotons snake their way along minor roads on Sundays. Road drainage appears uncommon in southern Italy, so avoid driving during rain. Road signage can be difficult to interpret so take some time to get it right. For example, a straight on sign often looks to be indicating left or right. If you need to stop and think about which way to go, putting your hazard lights on will be enough to encourage people to drive around you. The south of Italy is less busy than the north, but Italians love their cars so there is always some traffic. Appalling congestion occurs after supper because everybody with a car cruises around town so try to avoid driving between 7pm and 10pm. Perhaps the recession will encourage them to promenade instead.

There are rumours that the Italians are mad drivers with one hand always on the horn. OK, they are expressive with their horns, but it is an unofficial language that is easy to learn. One short beep from a following car is a warning that they are overtaking or simply 'I am here'. Two beeps means 'ciao' and they are generally saying hello to someone they know. A progression of beeps or one long beeeeeeeep usually means you or something else is in the way; either they have nearly driven into you or there is a parked car blocking the route. Italians drive at two speeds, fast and slow. People driving slowly are happy to drift along and are not concerned by confused tourists. People in a hurry will drive with full beam lights on and will flash manically; as a general rule everyone gets out of their way.

Parking is an Italian sport and any space is fair game, even if it blocks the road. When confronted by a blocked road it is standard practice to give a long horn blast, shopkeepers and passersby soon inspect the situation then summon the owner to move the vehicle. Many cities do not allow tourist traffic through the historic centre, so park on the outskirts and use public transport to get in. Tailgating is something you have to accept.

Go Motorhoming and Campervanning

Some ski resorts can only be accessed by crossing high mountain passes that are prone to blockages after light snow and wind. All tourist offices receive daily updates about mountain-pass conditions and a three-day snow forecast. Winter tyres are required between October 15th and April 15th.

If you have a bike rack or anything that protrudes from the rear of your motorhome, ensure you identify it with a hazard warning sign. These are 50cm square, with red and white reflective stripes.

LPG is widely available. Fuel stations may discount fuel prices at weekends, and self-service pumps are marked 'Fai Dante' and are often five per cent cheaper.

Portugal

Portugal has a relaxed pace of life that follows the seasons. Agricultural vehicles of all types are used as daily transport, testament to the family farm lifestyle so prevalent in the interior. During winter the Atlantic coast is often windier and wetter than the more sheltered Algarve; unsurprisingly, this is where most motorhomes congregate. If you drive north, away from the Sun-Seekers, you will find the wetlands around Aveiro. This area provides shellfish for birds and fishermen alike who navigate the creeks in traditional colourful fishing boats.

Sao Jacinto, Portugal.

Where To Stay

Portugal has approximately 250 campsites, many of which are open all year. 119 campsites are listed on www.campingportugal.org and 146 are listed on www.visitportugal.com. The publication *Roteiro Campista Camping Portugal* details 220 Portuguese campsites. This guidebook is available from tourist offices in Portugal.

There are 80 Motorhome Stopovers listed in *All the Aires Spain and Portugal,* most of which are located inland. Offsite-Parking is possible but 'No Motorhome' signs are common along the coast.

Driving And Roads
Compared to Spanish roads, Portuguese roads are in poor condition and country lanes are very bumpy. Main roads are busy and the surface has often deteriorated and is potholed. The local driving style is calm, and the local roads are quiet. Portuguese toll roads have a 12-hour time restriction. As always the advice, for safety reasons, is do not park overnight at motorway rest areas, but in this case, time is also against you. Electronic tolls, signed 'Lanco Com Portagem', apply on many of the formerly free stretches of motorway. This is an automated system and there are no tollbooths. Instead, an electronic device has to be leased or a three-day ticket can be purchased. These are available from motorway service stations and at borders and must be acquired before you use the motorways. Visit http://portagens.ctt.pt or see the tourist board website.

LPG is available in Portugal at many fuel stations, www.autogas.pt. Fuel is 10 cents more per litre in Portugal than it is in Spain.

Spain
Southern coastal Spain provides the warmest winter temperatures in mainland Europe, thus motorhome and caravan users migrate there from all over the continent. The warm winters make it viable to grow a wide selection of fruits, vegetables, and salad crops. The evidence of this intensive production is clearly visible as thousands of hectares of southern Spain are cloaked in plastic. To experience a quieter and more beautiful Spain drive inland across the mountain plains.

View from N340, Spain.

Go Motorhoming and Campervanning

Where To Stay
Spain has 1,200 campsites. There are many large campsites located along the southeastern coast that are suitable for long term winter holidays. Rallies are held at these campsites by motorhome and caravan clubs from all over Europe. The publication *Guia Camping,* details campsites in Spain and Portugal and has a searchable database of campsites on the supporting website, www.guiacampingfecc.com.

There are 160 Motorhome Stopovers in Spain. Almost half are located above Portugal, between the Atlantic coast and San Sebastián. Most of these stopovers are located inland, and are underused despite being free and open all year. Full details are provided in *All the Aires Spain and Portugal* available from www.vicarious-shop.com. If you dream of driving slowly down the Spanish Mediterranean coast and stopping wherever takes your fancy, you are going to be disappointed. Offsite-Parking is nearly non-existent as more and more motorhome exclusion signs are erected, and you are unlikely to find a free Motorhome Stopover near the sea.

Unfortunately, there is an element of crime targeted at tourists. Many campsites display warning and disclaimer notices about leaving belongings outside and valuables on display when you are away from your pitch. Spanish highway police on the AP7 confirmed that break-ins both on trucks and motorhomes were a real problem at motorway rest areas, but rarely occur off the motorway network. Do not stop overnight at motorway service or rest areas and be vigilant at all times when visiting them.

Driving And Roads
In general, Spanish roads are the best in Europe having recently been subject to an extensive EU road improvement programme. Although this has made Spanish roads easy and pleasant to drive on, it can cause navigation issues for both humans and satellite machines. Ensure you have up-to-date mapping with you. Away from major cities the local driving style is generally non-aggressive, cautious, and very tolerant. Toll roads along the east coast connect the popular coastal resorts. There are also reasonable free roads that follow the same route. This coast is very busy and is virtually all built-up. Driving the central route up or down is quiet, beautiful and toll free.

Speed detectors linked to traffic lights are common at town boundaries. The traffic lights stop speeding vehicles before they enter the built up areas. Spanish road planners have adopted a type of junction which would be a roundabout elsewhere in Europe. To prevent vehicles turning left across the traffic a right hand slipway sweeps away and back at right angles to the road. Drivers then have to give way to traffic on both carriageways. This type of junction is likely to be traffic light controlled in towns. These junctions can be unexpected so look for them!

Almost a roundabout in Spain.

 LPG is available at 30 sites, see www.repsolypf.com and www.aoglp.com. The majority of Spanish LPG outlets are detailed in *All the Aires Spain and Portugal.*

United Kingdom

The UK is probably the most diverse country in Europe and there is so much to see and do that a lifetime of weekends and holidays can easily be filled. Visiting country houses and historical industrial buildings will give you a good understanding of how the people that shaped the UK's countryside and industry lived. Members of the National Trust, www.nationaltrust.org.uk, and English Heritage, www.english-heritage.org.uk, have free access to hundreds of historic buildings and places of interest. You can join at one of the more popular sites so there is no need to take out membership in advance. National Trust members also have access to buildings owned by the National Trust for Scotland www.nts.org.uk. The National Trust offers free entry to members of affiliated overseas National Trusts, so bring your membership card if you are a member in: Australia, New Zealand, Barbados, Bermuda, Canada, Jersey, Guernsey, or the Isle of Man. Camping is practical all year in England and Wales

Thorpeness, Suffolk.

because of the mild climate, but it is best to tour from April to October to avoid dreary winter weather and cold spells. Cornwall, Ireland and Wales are the wettest regions of the UK. Scotland is a bit too cold for winter camping, so plan a summer visit. Be warned mosquitoes are a problem.

Where To Stay

There are 2,400 campsites in the UK and a wide network of independent campsites are detailed in numerous campsite guides available from www.vicarious-shop.com. There are several UK campsite directories online. Unfortunately, the UK does not have a network of Motorhome Stopovers, but does have about 4,000 mini camping farm sites with pitch fees as low as £3.50 per night. The easy way to gain access to these mini camping sites is to join one of the camping clubs. The Camping and Caravanning Club allows caravans, motorhomes and tents on its campsites. See www.campingandcaravanningclub.co.uk, Tel: 02476 475442. Membership gives access to 110 club sites and 1,500 certified sites (mini camping). Many of the larger club sites are open to non-member visitors, who pay the full rate. Annual membership costs £40 and temporary three-month membership is available to foreign nationals for £20. Membership can be taken out at club sites. Members of The Caravan Club can camp in caravans and motorhomes at 200 club sites, including Crystal Palace in London and 2,500 small certified locations (mini camping). Annual membership costs £43 and it is possible to join at any club site. See www.caravanclub.co.uk, Tel: 01342 326944.

Certified Locations/Sites (CL/CS) are restricted to a maximum of five member caravans/motorhomes per night. These sites are located at farms, pubs and in people's gardens, so you are able to experience true UK culture in otherwise inaccessible areas. Every site offers water and a waste disposal facility, some offer electricity and showers. Information about these locations is provided in the clubs handbooks and on their websites.

There are so few official Motorhome Stopovers in the UK that you could publish information about them on two sides of A4 paper. Visit www.UKmotorhomes.net for a current list. Five hundred pubs allow members of a UK scheme called 'Motorhome Stopovers' to stop for the night. Membership costs £30 per year and members have access to the pub database on www.motorhomestopover.co.uk. There is another UK scheme called Brit Stops that emulates *France passion,* see www.britstops.com for details. Although by-laws generally exclude Offsite-Parking, in practice, it is possible to Offsite-Park in the UK if you stop late and leave early, but avoid the obvious tourist hot spots and the coast. Pub landlords and farmers will often let you stop for the night if asked nicely. Some Scottish Islands allow Offsite-Parking, but check with the local tourist office first.

Driving And Roads

Remember to drive on the left. Britain has some of the busiest roads in Europe and most towns in the Southeast and the Midlands experience rush hour congestion from 8am-9am and 5pm-6pm. Rural counties experience less congestion. The M25 around London can come to a standstill at any time as can the toll free M6 near Birmingham. Despite local opinion, the roads in the UK are good and most are free to use, apart from toll bridges crossing major estuaries and the M6 toll road around Birmingham.

There are about 2,000 low bridges in the UK. Bridge heights and road widths are often shown only in feet and inches, not metres. Make sure you convert your vehicle's measurements into feet and keep it on display in the cab. Truckers' maps, showing bridge heights, are available at service stations. Country lanes are narrow and often two-way. Roads in the West Country and Wales can be very narrow and busy during the tourist season; be prepared to use the pull-ins provided or reverse if necessary.
London has both a low emission zone, www.tfl.gov.uk/lezlondon, and a congestion charge, www.tfl.gov.uk/roadusers/congestioncharging. There is no need to drive through London and it is easier, and probably cheaper, to stay overnight outside of the zones and use public transport to get in.

LPG is available in the UK, but not from every fuel station. A map of LPG stations is displayed at www.drivelpg.co.uk/map/index.php.

The Crown Dependencies Of Jersey, Guernsey And The Isle Of Man

There are three Crown Dependency islands: Jersey, Guernsey, and the Isle of Man, none of these islands is part of the EU. Jersey and Guernsey are located off the coast of France. Motorhomes are accepted as long as campsites are pre-booked. Sea crossings must be made with Condor Ferries and motorhomes cannot exceed 7m in length. More information can be found at www.visitguernsey.com and www.jersey.com. The Isle of Man is located between Ireland and Wales and is accessible via ferry from both the UK and Ireland. There are 19 campsites listed on the tourist board website, www.visitisleofman.com.

Europe-Wide Additional Information

Country	EU Member	Schengen Zone	Currency	Emergency phone numbers	Tourist infomation
Albania	X	X	Leke	Dial; 129 for Police, 128 for fire, 127 for Ambulance (taxis may be quicker!)	www.albaniantourism.com
Andorra	X	X	Euro	Police; 110, Fire and Ambulance; 118, Emergency Medical service; 112	www.andorra.ad
Austria	Y	Y	Euro	Dial 112 in an emergency	www.austria.info/uk
Belarus	X	X	Ruble	Dial; 102 for Police, 101 for fire, 103 for Ambulance	http://eng.belarustourism.by
Belgium	Y	Y	Euro	Dial 112 in an emergency	www.belgiumtheplaceto.be (Wallonia), www.visitflanders.co.uk (Flanders)
Bosnia Herzegovnia	X	X	Konvertibilna Marka	Dial; 122 for Police, 123 for fire, 124 for Ambulance	http://www.bhtourism.ba/
Bulgaria	Y	X	Lev	Dial 112 in an emergency	www.bulgariatravel.org www.travel-bulgaria.com
Croatia	X	X	Kuna	Dial 112 in an emergency	www.croatia.hr
Czech Republic	Y	X	Crown	Dial 112 in an emergency	www.czechtourism.com
Denmark	Y	Y	Krone (DKK)	Dial 112 in an emergency	www.visitdenmark.com
Estonia	Y	Y	Euro	Dial 112 in an emergency	www.visitestonia.com or www.tourism.ee
Finland	Y	Y	Euro	Dial 112 in an emergency	www.visitfinland.com
France	Y	Y	Euro	Dial 112 in an emergency	www.franceguide.com
Germany	Y	Y	Euro	Dial 112 in an emergency	www.germany-tourism.co.uk
Greece	Y	Y	Euro	Dial 112 in an emergency	www.visitgreece.gr Tel: 020 4959 3000
Hungary	Y	Y	Euro	Dial 112 in an emergency	www.gotohungary.co.uk
Iceland	X	Y	Krona	Dial 112 in an emergency	www.visiticeland.com
Ireland	Y	X	Euro	Dial 112 in an emergency	www.ireland.ie, www.discoverireland.com
Italy	Y	Y	Euro	Dial 112 in an emergency	www.visititaly.com
Kosovo	X	X	Euro	Dial 112 in an emergency	www.visitkosovo.org and http://beinkosovo.com
Latvia	Y	Y	Lat	Dial 112 in an emergency	www.latvia.travel

Country			Currency	Emergency	Website
Lithuania	Y	Y	Litas	Dial 112 in an emergency	www.leituva.lt/en/tourism
Luxembourg	Y	Y	Euro	Dial 112 in an emergency	www.visitluxembourg.lu
Macedonia (Republic of)	X	X	Denar	Dial 112 in an emergency	www.exploringmacedonia.com
Malta	Y	Y	Euro	Dial 112 in an emergency	www.visitmalta.com
Montenegro (Republic of)	X	X	Euro	Dial 112 in an emergency	www.visit-montenegro.com
Morocco	X	X	Dirham	Dial; 117 for Police, 15 for Fire, 15 for Ambulance	www.visitmorocco.com or www.morocco.com
Netherlands	Y	Y	Euro	Dial 112 in an emergency	www.visitholland.com
Norway	X	Y	Kroner (NOK)	Dial; 110 for fire, 112 for Police and 113 for Ambulance	www.visitnorway.com
Poland	Y	Y	Zloty	Dial 112 in an emergency	www.poland.travel
Portugal	Y	Y	Euro	Dial 112 in an emergency	www.visitportugal.com
Romania	Y	X	Leu	Dial 112 in an emergency	www.romaniatourism.com
Russian Federation	X	X	Rouble	Dial 112 in an emergency	www.visitrussia.org.uk
Serbia (Republic of)	X	X	Dinar	Dial 112 in an emergency	www.serbia.travel
Slovakia	Y	Y	Euro	Dial 112 in an emergency	www.slovakia.org
Slovinia	Y	Y	Euro	Dial 112 in an emergency	www.slovenia.info
Spain	Y	Y	Euro	Dial 112 in an emergency	www.spain.info
Sweden	Y	Y	Krona	Dial 112 in an emergency	www.visitsweden.com
Switzerland	X	Y	Swiss franc	Dial; 117 for Police, 118 for Fire, 144 for Ambulance and 1414 for Swiss Rescue	www.myswitzerland.com
Turkey	X	X	Lira	Dial; 115 for Police, 110 for Fire, 112 for Ambulance	www.gototurkey.co.uk
Ukraine	X	X	Hryvnia	Dial; 02 for Police, 01 for fire, 03 for Ambulance	www.traveltoukraine.org
United Kingdom	Y	X	Pound (Sterling)	Dial 999 or 112 in an emergency	www.visitbritain.com

European Driving Speed Limits And Regulations By Vehicle Weight For Motorhomes And Caravans

European Country	MAM (Maximum Authorised Weight of Tow Vehicle or Motorhome)	Built-up Areas (Citys, Towns, Villages)	Single Carriageways, Lanes, Trunk Routes, Bypasses, Single-Track Roads, Highways	Dual Carriagewways, Expresssways	Motorways, Autoroutes, Autobahn, Autostrada	Trailer, Caravan, A-frame Restrictions	Other Speed and Weight Restrictions in Europe
Andorra	-	50kmh	60kmh	90kmh	-	-	-
Austria	<3,500kg	50kmh	100kmh	-	130kmh	80kmh (S) and 100kmh (M)	
	>3,500kgs	-	70kmh	-	80kmh	-	
Belarus		60kmh	90kmh	-	120kmh	-	Vehicles >3500kg cannot drive in left lane on roads with 3+ lanes.
Belgium	<7,500kg	50kmh	90kmh	-	120kmh	-	
	>7,500kg	-	60kmh	-	90kmh	-	
Bosnia Herzegovina	-	50kmh	80kmh	-	130kmh	-	
Bulgaria	<3,500kg	50kmh	90kmh	-	130kmh	-	
	>3,500kg	-	70kmh	-	100kmh	-	
Croatia	-	50kmh	80kmh	-	100kmh	80kmh (S) and 90kmh (M)	
Cyprus	-	50kmh	80kmh	-	100kmh	-	
Czech Republic	<3,500kg	50kmh	80kmh	90kmh	130kmh	80kmh	
	>3,500kg	50kmh	80kmh	-	80kmh	-	
Denmark	<3,500kg	50kmh	80kmh	90kmh	130kmh	70kmh (S) and 80kmh (M)	
	>3,500kg	-	70kmh	-	70kmh	-	
Estonia	<3,500kgs	50kmh	90kmh	-	110kmh	-	
	>3,500kg <7,500kg	-	70kmh	-	90kmh	-	
Finland	Motorhomes up to 3,500kg	50kmh	80kmh	80kmh	100kmh	70kmh (S) and 80kmh (M)	
	Motorhomes over 3,500kg	50kmh	80kmh	80kmh	80kmh	-	
France	<3,500kg	50kmh	90kmh	110kmh	130kmh	-	
	>3,500kg	50kmh	80kmh	90kmh	90kmh	-	

< = Less than; > = More than. (S) = Single Carriageway. (M) = Motorway.
*Higher speed limit applies to trailers/caravans with braking systems. Lower speed applies to trailers/caravans, without braking systems.

Country	Weight						Notes
Germany	<3,500kg	50kmh	100kmh	-	130kmh	80kmh	
	>3,500kg <7500kg	50kmh	80kmh	-	100kmh	60kmh	
	>7,500kg	50kmh	80kmh	-	80kmh	-	
Gibraltar	-	50kmh	50kmh	-	50kmh	-	
Great Britain	-	30mph (48)	60mph (96)	70mph (112)	50mph (S), 70mph (112)	60mph (D+M)	No trailers in the right-hand lane of a motorway with three or more lanes.
	>3,050kg unlaiden weight	30mph (48)	50mph (80)	60mph (96)	70mph (112)	-	
Greece	-	50kmh	90kmh	110kmh	130kmh	80kmh	
Hungary	<2,500kg	50kmh	90kmh	110kmh	130kmh	80kmh	
	>2,500kg	50kmh	70kmh	-	80kmh	-	
Iceland	-	50kmh	80kmh	-	90kmh	-	Highways are defined as gravel roads and motorways as asphalt roads.
Ireland	-	50kmh	100kmh	-	120kmh	-	
Italy	<3,500kg	50kmh	90kmh	110kmh	130kmh	70kmh (S) and 80kmh (M)	
	>3,500kg	50kmh	80kmh	-	100kmh	-	
Latvia	<2,800kg	50kmh	90kmh	-	110kmh	-	
	>2,800kg <7,500kg	50kmh	90kmh	-	90kmh	-	
Lithuania	<3,500kg	60kmh	90kmh	-	110kmh	-	
	>3,500kg <7,500kg	60kmh	70kmh	-	-	-	
Luxembourg	<3,500kg	50kmh	90kmh	-	130kmh	75kmh (S) and 90kmh (M)	
	>3,500kg	40kmh	75kmh	-	90kmh	-	
Macedonia	-	60kmh	80kmh	-	120kmh	-	
Montenegro	-	50kmh	80kmh	-	100kmh	-	
Netherlands	-	50kmh	80kmh	100kmh	120kmh	80kmh (S) and 90kmh (M)	
	>3,500kg	50kmh	80kmh	80kmh	80kmh	-	
Norway	<3,500kg	50kmh	80kmh	90kmh	100kmh	60kmh or 80kmh*	
	>3,500kg <7,500kg	50kmh	80kmh	-	80kmh	-	

Continued overleaf

European Country	MAM (Maximum Authorised Weight of Tow Vehicle or Motorhome)	Built-up Areas (Citys, Towns, Villages)	Single Carriageways, Lanes, Trunk Routes, Bypasses, Single-Track Roads, Highways	Dual Carriageways, Expressways	Motorways, Autoroutes, Autobahn, Autostrada	Trailer, Caravan, A-frame Restrictions	Other Speed and Weight Restrictions in Europe
Poland	<3,500kg	50kmh	90kmh	110kmh	130kmh	70kmh (S) and 80kmh (M)	
	>3,500kg	50kmh	70kmh	-	80kmh	-	
Portugal	<3,500kg	50kmh	90kmh	100kmh	120kmh	-20kmh	
	>3,500kg	50kmh	90kmh	-	110kmh	-	
Romania	<3,500kg	50kmh	90kmh	-	100kmh	-	
	>3,500kg	50kmh	80kmh	-	90kmh	-	
Russia	-	60kmh	90kmh	-	110kmh	-	
Serbia/ Montenegro	<3,500kg	50kmh	100kmh	-	120kmh	-	
	>3,500kg	50kmh	80kmh	-	80kmh	-	
Slovakia	<3,500kg	50kmh	90kmh	-	130kmh	90kmh	
	>3,500kg <6,000kg	50kmh	80kmh	80kmh	90kmh	-	
Slovenia	<3,500kg	50kmh	90kmh	100kmh	130kmh	80kmh	
	>3,500kg	50kmh	80kmh	80kmh	80kmh	-	
Spain	Cars	50kmh	90kmh	100kmh	120kmh	70kmh (S) and 80kmh (M)	<7500kg trailers 80kmh (S) and 90kmh (M)
	Motorhomes of any weight	50kmh	70kmh	80kmh	100kmh	70kmh (S) and 80kmh (M)	<7500kg trailers 80kmh (S) and 90kmh (M)
Sweden	<3,500kg	50kmh	70kmh	100kmh	120kmh	50kmh or 80kmh*	
	>3,500kg	50kmh	80kmh	-	100kmh	-	
Switzerland	<3,500kg	50kmh	80kmh	100kmh	120kmh	80kmh	Towing cars on motorways is only permitted up to the next exit at a maximum speed of 40kmh.
Turkey	-	50kmh	80kmh	-	100kmh	-	
	>3,500kg	50kmh	90kmh	-	120kmh	110kmh	
Ukraine	-	60kmh	110kmh	-	130kmh	-	

< = Less than; > = More than. (S) = Single Carriageway. (M) = Motorway.
*Higher speed limit applies to trailers/caravans with braking systems. Lower speed applies to trailers/caravans, without braking systems.
Please ensure you are up to date on local laws and driving regulations before travelling to any foreign country and always adhere to road signs while driving abroad.

Now that you are an armchair expert, you are ready to take the next step with confidence. If you already own a motorhome, book a crossing, pack your guidebooks, then go and enjoy the freedom of motorhoming. Motorhome virgins should rent or buy something affordable that is a manageable size.

Remember that a motorhome is not a pet and can be just for Christmas. As we explained, the perfect motorhome does not exist. During your first few trips, you discover whether you are willing to compromise accessibility and manoeuvrability over living space.

Before you depart, make sure that you have packed the essential items listed in Chapter 2. Ignore for now, any must-have gadgets and gizmos and reconsider them once you have cut your teeth. Make sure your administration is in order and fit a safe so that you can keep your passports, important documents, and valuables under lock and key. Ensure that you pack enough of your favourite teabags to last your trip; spices are also hard to find on the continent. Remember to weigh your motorhome once everything is packed.

We have explained what to expect from the different accommodation options and you know how to be a responsible motorhome tourist. We recommend that you sample everything that is on offer so that you can find out for yourself what type of motorhomer you are. Use the country guides to help you decide where to go and explore.

> **Chris's top tip:** Buy a motorhome no longer than 6m that weighs no more than 3,500kg.
>
> **Meli's top tip:** Do not worry about the destination simply plan your trips around the things you want to see and do.
>
> **Vicarious Books top tip:** Knowledge is power and ignorance is avoidable so pack your maps, tourist, hobby, and stopover guidebooks before you depart.
>
> **Vicarious Books cat:** Don't forget you dogs and cats need a PETS passport.

Updates and amendments to this book are provided on www.go-motorhoming.co.uk. We welcome your comments, experiences and updates.

Thaon les Vosges canal side Aire, France.

Taule Penze.

A

B